ANNE BRADSTREET'S
QUEST FOR SPIRITUAL SOLACE

ANNE BRADSTREET'S
QUEST FOR SPIRITUAL SOLACE

Selected Poems

Nasser Al-Beshri

Copyright © 2012 by Nasser Al-Beshri.

Library of Congress Control Number:		2012911357
ISBN:	Hardcover	978-1-4771-3235-7
	Softcover	978-1-4771-3234-0
	Ebook	978-1-4771-3236-4

All rights reserved. No part of this book may be reproduced or transmitted in any form or by any means, electronic or mechanical, including photocopying, recording, or by any information storage and retrieval system, without permission in writing from the copyright owner.

To order additional copies of this book, contact:
Xlibris Corporation
1-800-618-969
www.Xlibris.com.au
Orders@Xlibris.com.au
501897

Contents

Acknowledgments..7
Abstract..9
Introduction..11

Chapter One:
 Anne Bradstreet's Life and the Puritan Belief 17

Chapter Two:
 Bradstreet's Inner Struggle: "The Flesh and the Spirit".........25

Chapter Three:
 Bradstreet's Joys and Sorrows: "In Memory of My Dear Grandchild Elizabeth Bradstreet," "Verses upon the Burning of Our House," and "To My Dear and Loving Husband"..35

Chapter Four:
 Life is a Journey: "As Weary Pilgrim"......................................57

Conclusion 67
Bibliography..71
Index..79

Acknowledgments

Praise be to God, Almighty, Who gave me the ability to produce this work. O Lord! I cannot praise You enough for the countless blessings You have bestowed upon me.

I would like to present my sincere gratitude to Prof. A. R. Kutrieh, may he rest in peace, for teaching and introducing me to such a great poet whose works have inspired me. More importantly, special and deep thanks to my supervisor during the MA program, Prof. Syed Asim Ali, for his thorough and insightful remarks and for the countless hours he spent teaching and guiding me. Without his help, this book would never have been the way it is now.

I cannot forget to thank my parents, may God bless them, who have been teaching me how to be a better person: hard-working, honest, and kind to others. They made me the man I am. I hope they are proud of me. Finally, special thanks to my dear wife and to my son, Abdullah, the best thing that ever happened to me in this life; thank you for making my life pleasant and sorry for all the time I have been away from you. I wish things were different!

Abstract

This book studies Anne Bradstreet's quest for spiritual solace during times of hardships after she and her family fled from England to North America. During those adversities, Bradstreet questioned her faith. In all the poems subject of this book Bradstreet's inner struggle between her flesh and spirit can obviously be seen. Bradstreet uses her talent in poetry writing as a means to express her thoughts and fears hoping to find the peace and comfort she needs. Bradstreet was able to get over all those shattering hardships and emerge a better person believing even more strongly than ever that God will reward her patience in the afterlife with better and heavenly blessings. Before her death, the constant disturbing struggle between her flesh and spirit is replaced by serenity and longing for heaven.

INTRODUCTION

Anne Bradstreet (1612-1672) is an early American Puritan female poet whose poetry transcended time and place. She has received a great deal of attention, especially, during the last half century. Bradstreet was born in the house of the Earl of Lincoln, whom her father, Thomas Dudley, served as a steward. Anne with her brother and sisters enjoyed the luxury of living in the Lincolnshire countryside and benefited from the Earl's library as well as from the surrounding Puritan spiritual atmosphere. Puritanism was a reforming branch of Christianity whose apparent aim was to return to the early simplicity of Christianity. Anne also enjoyed the company of her well-educated father and his educated friend, Simon Bradstreet, whom she married later on when she was sixteen. In 1630, the Dudleys and the Bradstreets, with many other Puritans fled to New England in America with John Winthrop to establish the Massachusetts Bay Colony, which they hoped would be a utopian state in the Puritan sense. Anne Bradstreet lived in New England the rest of her life until she died at the age of sixty in Andover, Massachusetts.

According to Gordon Bradstreet is the first English-speaking poet in North America (*Mistress Bradstreet* x). She "revealed herself as a unique and striking individual against the backdrop of her times . . . [She is a] cultured, educated Englishwoman adapting herself to a totally strange new environment, a loving wife, a devoted mother, a questing Puritan, and a sensitive poet" (Laughlin 1). The study of Bradstreet's poetry is of great value in that it provides an insight into her poetic characteristics and psychology in particular as one of the new settlers in North America. Avery R. Fischer argues that Bradstreet can be categorized as either an early feminist poet whose heart rose in resistance to the social order or a seventeenth-century Puritan pious person, thanks to many of her poems in which she decides "to resign herself to God's will" (11). The life and works of Anne Bradstreet have been approached differently; however, few studies have paid due attention to the late and more personal elegies of Anne Bradstreet *vis-a-vis* her personal life experiences. The study of one of her late and more personal elegies, "To My Dear and Loving Husband," one of her marriage poems "In Memory of my Dear Grandchild Elizabeth Bradstreet, who Deceased August, 1665, Being a Year and Half Old," and her poems "The Flesh and the Spirit," "Verses Upon the Burning of Our House," and "As Weary Pilgrim" may help explore her deep feelings and personality, and discover her inner struggle between worldly pleasures and spiritual quest. This book will also attempt to discover how Bradstreet was able to find spiritual solace. It will lead deep into the essential fabric of her poetic ideas and themes. Almost all of her poems, subject of this study, exist in all American poetry anthologies. Scholars such as: Ann Stanford, Elizabeth Wade White, Adrianne Rich, Josephine Piercy, Rosamond Rosenmeier, and many others have dedicated biographical and scholarly books that discuss her life and works.

Bradstreet was one of those new settlers of New England, the Puritans, who shared amongst themselves a number of typical characteristics; they were religious, honest, sincere, and determined to achieve their goals and fight for their cause, which was to establish a new world where everything is perfect. Their journey from the European continent to North America was in a way symbolic of a Catholic's journey to Jerusalem. They fled England because they were persecuted by the British monarchy and thus the New Settlers sought refuge in the wilderness of their new settlement abroad. Unfortunately and ironically, the victim was to become a victimizer in the course of time; the new settlers abused the power they had over the native Indians in their New World and deprived them of their old home. However, the focus of my study, which is the poetry of Anne Bradstreet, is of great significance since it provides a better understanding of her personal and poetic traits as well as her inner struggle between flesh and spirit, in particular, and the individuality of the new settlers in the New World in general. The early settlers of America were a group of people strengthened by their determination to build an independent state where they could practice their religion freely. Bradstreet was a member of that society. The secret of the new settlers' success can be discovered in Bradstreet's poetry. This study will try to grasp some of the factors that led to the success of the new settlers by deciphering them in Bradstreet's poetry.

It is to be studied if it was Bradstreet's strong faith in religion and her unflinching spirituality that enabled her to overcome all her doubts about the divine plan preordained for her, believing that she will be rewarded for her faith with an everlasting bliss in the hereafter. This was probably the secret of her inner strength that bestowed upon her spiritual peace and comfort in her life in the face of a number of unnerving adversities and crises. This kind of attitude was rooted probably in her Puritan upbringing. This study explores this point in deeper details and tries to see the impact of the Puritan belief on her poetry and character.

Bradstreet's poetry represents the Puritan thought and dogma in the main. Her poetry tells a great deal about herself; she reveals about herself more than she could have intended. In her poems she uses a certain distinguished style and imagery to express her ideas and feelings. Her style is simple, direct, smooth, and sincere. Moreover, it is lyrical and unique in themes, imagery, and style especially in her last and more mature poems. The diction and metaphors she employs are mostly gleaned from the Bible as well as from the natural landscapes surrounding her. A careful observer may notice that there runs a consistent streak of inner conflict between worldly and spiritual demands in most of her poetry; a conflict which is a recurrent motif. The struggle between her bodily desires and spiritual aspirations takes the form of a logical conflict or an argument that develops gradually until it always ends with her spiritual belief prevailing.

The inner struggle she experienced between her worldly desires and spiritual aspirations is most apparent in her poems "The Flesh and the Spirit," "Verses Upon the Burning of Our House," and in her later and more personal elegies. Man, since the time of Adam and Eve has continuously suffered from this inner conflict between his carnal desires and his spiritual demands. This inner struggle becomes more intense in times of predicaments. When people lose a loved one or something precious and dear to them, they protest in anger and may utter disapproval of the divinely ordained fate, at least in the heat of the moment. However, the submission to God's plan, no matter how sad or terrible the consequences may be, is a sign of strong faith. Bradstreet's inner struggle resulted from the death of her closest kith and kin and the burning of her house with all her personal belongings in it. The difficult living conditions she and the early settlers had to endure in the New World during early seventeenth century were a contributing factor. Her inner struggle came from her desire to compromise with God's will, which sometimes appeared unjust, and at the same time not to give up on life or protest in anger against God's will. The intensity of the calamity at times was such that a person of shaky faith might have acted against his/her beliefs. In her poetry, Bradstreet shows forth an example of strong faith—despite the destruction of her house, loss of her four grandchildren, and her daughter-in-law who was dear to her as her own child (and most were taken in quick succession). She accepts her destiny without serious grumble. Thus, she presents herself as an example of a fine, honorable, and diligent individual in New England firmly rooted in religiously inspired patience and fortitude.

Faith in Bradstreet's poetry seems to strengthen and enable her to overcome adversities. The same applies for individuals in other societies; faith can be a source that elevates their strength and self-esteem through spirituality. Materialistic societies are known for their suffering from spiritual hollowness. The same idea has been projected by some great poets, such as Wordsworth, Matthew Arnold, and T. S. Eliot. They condemn the materialistic attitudes in life and emphasize the importance of restoring spiritual faith and religious belief. Faithlessness may create a feeling of worthlessness in individuals that negatively influences their productivity. It can give them a feeling of insecurity, aimlessness, and insignificance. Consequently, uncertainty, fear, and indifference may dominate and give rise to chaos and corruption. Bradstreet seems to convey to the modern Man, through her sincerity, unflinching faith, resilience, and endurance, how to defeat adversity.

This study will illustrate how Anne Bradstreet in times of tests and tribulations tries in her poetry to seek spiritual solace with God. When she experienced crises, like the loss of a family member or the burning of her house, her faith in God was momentarily shaken. But for a Puritan, lack of faith is extremely unacceptable. This study will explain how Bradstreet used writing poetry as a means to comfort herself. In many of her poems and in poems under this study she uses the technique of logical argumentation in order to seek, gradually, self-rehabilitation and consequently strengthen her faith in God. This process of reaching spiritual harmony with God makes her stronger. Bradstreet is a role model for the successful and productive individuals in society; she was a good wife, mother, and grandmother. Continuing in these roles, she contributed poetry and prose to English literature, transforming thereby her personal experiences into universally appreciable artistic experiences. Thus, she succeeded in carving out for herself a niche as the first female English poet of worth.

This study, in the second chapter, will explore Bradstreet's inner conflict between the worldly desires and spiritual aspirations visible in most of her poetry. This conflict between materialism and spirituality reaches its climax and becomes most apparent in Bradstreet's poem "The Flesh and the Spirit"; the title itself is suggestive of her internal struggle. This conflict can also be seen in her late and more personal poems though with less intensity. Bradstreet's inner struggle between flesh and spirit is normally governed by the theological and social norms of her time. She chooses to suppress her worldly desires because she cannot violate the religious and social norms she subscribes to. Nevertheless, Bradstreet's strong faith and her love of God remains the main factor behind her virtuous conduct.

This study will, also, explore Bradstreet's style, imagery, and themes; which she uses in order to overcome her inner struggle and convey her feelings. I will also explore how Bradstreet uses certain types of imagery and themes in her poetry as a defense mechanism to overcome her crises and find order in a chaotic world. This study will examine how she achieves simplicity, directness, and smoothness in her poetic style, and whether or not her exuberant tone of sincerity in her poetry constitutes an escape route for her from the pressure of testing circumstances. The extent of originality in her style and freshness of diction and metaphors she employs therein will also be determined.

In the third chapter, this study will lay bare the secrets behind Bradstreet's fortitude in times of horrible familial crises and her affirmative role in society and family as a mother and wife by analyzing her "Verses Upon the Burning of Our House," "To My Dear and Loving Husband," and her late elegy to her grandchild, Elizabeth. Ann Stanford (19) says that from the Puritan point of view, family is very important unit for the state: the Massachusetts Bay Colony in Bradstreet's case. It is the basic unit that constitutes a state. Therefore, marriage is important for state and love is essential to matrimonial alliance. Bradstreet wrote her marriage poems in order to soothe and entertain herself during the long lonely cold nights while her husband was absent on public duty. Kenneth A. Requa says, while Bradstreet is writing her elegies for her grandchildren her intention is not to honor the 'deceased' but she rather "concerns herself primarily with reconciling . . . herself to the recent death" (*Poetic Voices* 4). The analysis of poems under this study will show how Bradstreet was able to accomplish her goals through poetry and resolve her inner conflict between her materialistic desires and spiritual goals.

The fourth chapter will also consider Bradstreet's perspective of life in her poem "As Weary Pilgrim." "As Weary Pilgrim" is a metaphor where Bradstreet compares life to a pilgrimage. This poem, Stanford says, is divided into two parts. The first is a simple one, in which Bradstreet compares herself to a pilgrim who passes through dangers and comes to the end of a long pilgrimage. The second part is a "resurrection to come," in the form of a "wedding song" that is "adapted to represent the union of Christ with his church or with the human soul" (Stanford 116). Life for Bradstreet is a journey. Her destination beyond life is Heaven. This philosophy of life explains Bradstreet's optimistic attitude in dealing with all crises she encountered in her life. She always looks up for unity with God and all the worldly pleasures and possessions are insignificant to her. However, her spirituality did not make her indifferent to her life in this world. She worked hard to build her society, family, and fame as a poet. In fact, her contribution to English literature in poetry and prose has continued to inspire her readers to this day.

Chapter One

Anne Bradstreet's Life and the Puritan Belief

This book will examine a selection of Anne Bradstreet's poetry in order to reach a better understanding and appreciation of her quest for spiritual solace. It will further try to link it to the secrets of her life that enabled her to stand aloft in the face of predicaments she had to encounter in her life. This chapter is a biographical background of Bradstreet in addition to some basic information about the Puritan ideology to which she subscribed in order to reach the aspired understanding of Bradstreet's poetry. However, this book is not intended to be mainly biographical. It is planned to be rather analytical in nature with focus on the aspects of her spiritual quest. For this purpose, a selection of her major poems will be subjected to thorough critical analysis in the chapters to follow.

Anne Dudley, who became Anne Bradstreet after she got married to Simon Bradstreet, was born in 1612 in Northampton, England. Her mother, Dorothy Yorke (1582-1643) was an educated gentlewoman. Her father, Thomas Dudley (1576-1653), was a courtier's page, an Elizabethan soldier and citizen, a Puritan partisan, and finally a deputy to the governor of the Massachusetts Bay Colony, John Winthrop, and then a governor himself. Thomas Dudley was converted to the Puritan belief by the Puritan preacher John Dod[1]. Dod, with many other prominent Puritan preachers, was outlawed from the practice of his profession; he was silenced for nonconformity. Dod was invited by his

---

[1] John Dod (1555-1645) was an accomplished theologian, trained at Jesus College, Cambridge, tireless in his calling and of a disciplined and holy way of life (Bush 310).

friend Sir Erasmus Dryden to Canons Ashby in Northamptonshire. It is likely that Dudley, who was living also in Northamptonshire within twenty miles from Canons Ashby, has attended Dod's services. It is, also, claimed that the Dudleys took their daughter Anne to be baptized by the revered minister there. There is no tangible evidence to prove that Anne was baptized in Canons Ashby because all documents before 1697 have disappeared, most likely as a result of the destruction caused by the Civil War between the Royalists and Parliamentarians.

In Canons Ashby, the great poet, "Edmund Spenser, a friend of Sir Erasmus,... (is) known to have been present at various times" exposing Anne Dudley as a child to his great poetry, which inspired her young and imaginative soul for poetry (White 4). Another significant Puritan figure, Thomas Lodge[2], visited the dowager Countess of Lincoln and inspired Anne and the learning atmosphere in the Countess household. Anne's education probably began in 1617, when she was five years old; and at the age of seven she had eight tutors in languages, music, and dancing and her father took great care to see that she received an education superior to that of all her peers. All young members of the Earl of Lincoln's Puritan household received a thoroughgoing religious education.

The Puritan crisis in England was the result of mainly two reasons: first, religious nonconformity; second, the refusal to pay taxes to King Charles I. The Puritans of the sixteenth and seventeenth century were advocating for a more 'pure' kind of worship. They believed that the English Church was tolerant of practices which they associated with the Catholic Church. During the reign of Queen Elizabeth I, they were active socially, religiously, and politically. Nonetheless, during the reign of King Charles I things changed dramatically for the Puritans. King Charles I was married to Henrietta-Marie de Bourbon of France, a zealous Roman Catholic. She was a Catholic extremist to the point that she did not attend the coronation of her husband because the ceremony was held in a non-Catholic Church. She evoked the feeling of animosity between the King and the Puritans. The "medieval principle of *un roi, une foi, une loi*—one king, one faith, one law—still held" influence on both Protestants and Catholics of that time (Gordon, *Mistress Bradstreet* 53). There was no tolerance for another faith in England. Religious men of all sects were fighting each other in the name of God. Unfortunately, to Christians, this bloody fight was a Medal of Honor and glory. The Puritans after being accused of religious nonconformity, in a largely Catholic country, had to flee for the sake of their own safety.

---

[2] Thomas Lodge (1558-1625) is an English writer and playwright and one of the University Wits (Bush 609).

The second reason was that King Charles I needed money to launch a war on Germany. Therefore, he started collecting taxes from the English people to finance his war campaign without consulting the parliament. As a result, six earls refused to pay; the Earl of Lincoln was one of them. Anne, at the age of seven or eight, moved in 1620 with her family from Northamptonshire to Lincolnshire to live in the household of Fiennes-Clinton family. The Earl of Lincoln is an important Puritan figure who was wanted for resisting the king's demand to pay taxes and was accused of religious nonconformity. All those who refused to pay the taxes to the king were mainly Puritans.

The Puritan resistance was the spark that started the fire of the Civil War and the formation of the Massachusetts Bay Company and the migration to New England. During that time most of the important Puritan figures "were either in prison or under summons to appear before the Privy Council" (White, *Anne Bradstreet* 86). Thomas Dudley was living in Boston, England and keeping a low profile until Sir Edward Herman, a Lincolnshire justice of the peace, sent a letter to the chancellor of the duchy of the Lancaster, Sir Humphrey May, telling him that Thomas Dudley was sheltering John Holland in his house. Holland was considered a fugitive of justice for religious nonconformity and not subscribing for the loan issued by the king. Because Thomas Dudley was wanted by the authorities, the marriage of his daughter Anne and Simon Bradstreet, a young graduate from Cambridge University, was held privately in the house of the Dudleys in Boston, England.

On March 23, 1628 the Massachusetts Bay Company was officially organized by a charter by the king of England to establish the first plantation in New England and other plantations to follow. The first voyage to New England was in the autumn of 1620 by the separatist Pilgrims who crossed the Atlantic Ocean in the *Mayflower* to form what was later known as the Plymouth colony. The second major voyage to New England took place through April and May of the year1629; Anne Bradstreet, her husband, and the Dudleys were all on that voyage. They were on the *Arabella*, the flag-ship of eleven other vessels carrying food, animals, and goods. In June 12, 1630 after seventy-seven days at sea, the *Arabella* arrived to the shores of New England, Salem. Thomas Dudley was chosen a deputy for the governor, John Winthrop.

After setting foot on land, the new settlers discovered that they were sick, exhausted, starving, with no town to entertain them or houses to shelter them from the brutal cold winter of New England or from the wild beasts, no hospitals to treat their patients, nothing but wild life. The Governor of the Plymouth Colony, William Bradford, in his journal *The Plymouth Plantation*, describes what they found on land when they crossed the "vast and furious ocean" to the New World on the *Mayflower* ship in 1620; he says: "what could they see but a hideous and desolate wilderness, full of wild beasts and wild men." He continues describing the weather as "fierce" and winter as "sharp and violent" (38). Anne Bradstreet was unhappy to leave the luxurious and civilized life of England. She expresses her doubts, unhappiness, and fear when she says that she "found a new world and new manners" at which "my heart rose" not in rejoice but in grief. She continues, "But after I was convinced that it was the way of God, I submitted" (Ellis 5). This proves how difficult it was for Bradstreet and other settlers to adjust to the new challenging environment; it was difficult to the point that she even doubted God. Yet, the greatest challenge the new settlers had "to stare down was not starvation, storms, plagues, whales, or even Indians. Instead it was the astonishing mystery they faced: Where were they going? What would it be like when they set foot on land?" (Gordon, *Mistress Bradstreet* 4). Having to face the unknown was their biggest challenge and fear. For the new settlers, it was similar to facing death. However, for the enterprising spirits it was an adventurous experience. The Elizabethans are famous for their thirst for adventure, exploration, power-seeking, and conquest.

In several places the mention of Indians is always associated with brutality and aggressiveness. Most writers describe them as being an obstacle or some sort of beasts that made the life of the new settlers harder and more dangerous. The story is always told from one (that is the settler's) point of view and it is summarily overlooked that it was their land that the new settlers had occupied and Indians were the victims. But the irony of the matter is that the victimizer portrays himself as the victim and the victim as victimizer; this happens when the powerful rules over the weak and when the judge is the enemy. However, there are some other writers, such as Benjamin Franklin, who treated the cause of Native Americans with just and understanding.

When the settlers of Salem came out to the shores to greet the new arrivals from homeland, the settlers of Salem were very sick and skinny to the point that their bones were visible under their paper-like skin. None of the settlers of Salem was able to build a house in the proper sense of a house. When Anne, her father, and John Winthrop went to get some rest at the best house in the colony; they found it was a dim and bleak wooden structure that consisted of two tiny rooms and two other rooms above. The best house of Salem looked like a small house of a poor peasant family in the countryside of England. Ironically, when the settlers in Salem ran out of food supplies, they had to rely on help from Indians and other plantations. Winthrop and Dudley knew that they could not stay in the miserable plantation of Salem but they had to establish their own colony. Therefore, they headed south to a deserted Indian settlement that was named Charleston by the settlers. The Bradstreets' first house in the New World barely protected them from the glazing sun and the stormy winds. Soon, Charleston, like every other plantation in the New World, became a miserable place where people died daily of starvation, and decimated by sickness. The settlers of Charleston were wretched and uncivilized. Anne was not used to this kind of lifestyle. In the aristocratic life she used to lead in England, she would never have to deal with the kind of people that lived in Charleston; they were uneducated workers, crude in their speech, and irreligious in their outlook on life.

In 1630, Thomas Dudley was running out of patience on the terrible conditions of Charleston. The Dudleys and the Bradstreets moved yet again from Charleston and settled in a new location. They built New Towne along a river, where the country's first college, Harvard, was built. In 1631, Thomas Dudley ordered a canal to be built from the river so they could deliver any type of goods, food, books, etc., to the doorstep of the inhabitants of New Towne. Life started to become easier and happier, and hope that God was watching over their shoulders to prosper in their life in the New World was by then something more realistic. In 1632, during the first winter in New Towne, Anne Bradstreet fell ill. She thought that she was going to die; however, when she recovered she became a stronger Puritan for she believed that God had sent that illness because of her doubts. She wrote, during her illness, her first poem: "Upon a Fit of Sickness."

In early 1633, Anne Bradstreet had her first child, Samuel. When Samuel was one-year old, his grandfather, Thomas Dudley, was elected to replace Winthrop as a governor of the Massachusetts Colony. Now both Dudley and Simon Bradstreet had to bear the heavy political, social, religious, and economic responsibilities of their colony. Anne must have heard them discussing their worries in her house. The first trouble Dudley had to handle was caused by his old friend, Roger Williams. Williams was a zealot who called for total separation from England. He went too far in his call for 'purity' and claimed that the Boston Church was not righteous because they still paid allegiance to King Charles I. Rumors that England might invade Boston were spreading and Williams was making things worse. Dudley, Winthrop, and the other magistrates could not allow Williams to do more harm; they had an order issued by the court that banned him from the colony.

After Williams's departure, Dudley and the colonists were hoping for some peace, but soon another troublemaker came to the shores of the Massachusetts Colony, it was Anne Hutchinson. She came to America to follow her favorite preacher and mentor John Cotton. She describes his words in utterly hyperbolic terms; that is, as if God was talking to her; she was that extreme. Her reputation as a wise and talented woman preceded her. Soon after her arrival, she became very active in society and soon she had over sixty women gathering in her house. She told them that the sermons of any preacher were not worth listening to, except sermons delivered by her spiritual mentor, Cotton. Therefore, whenever any other preacher, especially John Wilson, spoke in the meetinghouse, all women would leave or direct insulting gazes toward him. All these disturbing events were making Dudley more impatient with the government work. He was ready to leave for another new place, especially when most resources in New Towne started to dwindle away. Dudley was looking for a place where he will never have to worry about the beliefs of his children being corrupted by people like Williams or Hutchinson.

John Winthrop Jr. while hiking with a group of his friends found this perfect place for a new plantation, Ipswich. He took his wife there and built a small house for their small family. Ipswich was forty miles north of Boston and eighteen north of Salem. Unfortunately his wife soon died there. Dudley believed that in Ipswich he will take the burden of the government off his back. He was hoping for a distant place from the sins and impurity of the other plantations. The only eleven homes in Ipswich were the families of Simon's old Cambridge friends and other magistrates. They were rich and educated people with libraries full of books, to Anne's delight. Dudley, Simon, and the rest of the inhabitants of Ipswich were there for the same reason: more land and more distance from the disturbance of the colonies.

Soon Ipswich became as active as New Towne; the stream of emigrants from England never stopped until the English Civil War broke between King Charles I and the Puritans in England. Many new settlers came to live in Ipswich and the other colonies of New England; by the end of the 1630s, they were over fifty thousand colonists. Dudley was a restless soul always searching for true Puritanism trying to make the Massachusetts Bay Colony the Promised Land. In 1639, after he was reelected the deputy governor, he decided to move closer to Boston. Simon was more like his father-in-law, seeking remote land to seek true Puritanism. In 1646, the Bradstreets moved fifteen miles west from Ipswich to Andover and more precisely to a place called Cochichawicke, which was a fertile place that John Winthrop Jr. had bought from an Indian for six pounds and a coat. Anne and her sister, Mercy, along with their families moved together with the dream of building a new utopian Puritan settlement.

When Anne Bradstreet left Ipswich at the age of thirty-four, pregnant with the sixth child, she had just finished writing the four poems of *The Quaternions*: "The Four Elements," "Of the Four Humor," "The Four Ages of Man," and "The Four Seasons." These poems echo lines from the poetry of the French poet Sieur du Bartas (1540-90) who wrote a long verse-description of the creation of the world that was published in Paris in two parts, *La Sepmaine* in the year 1578 and *La Seconde Sepmaine* in 1584. Joshua Sylvester[3] translated

---

[3] Joshua Sylvester (1563-1618) is an influential English poet. It is claimed that Milton's *Paradise Lost* owes something to Sylvester's *Bartas: His Devine Weekes and Works* (Bush 73-75).

Du Bartas' whole work in *Bartas: His Devine Weekes and Works* (1605). This book became popular rapidly, several editions were printed; Sidney, Milton, and Anne Bradstreet reflect Bartas' influence at several places in their poetry.

In 1650 John Woodbridge, Bradstreet's brother-in-law, published her first book *The Tenth Muse Lately Sprung Up in America*. Whether she gave him permission to publish her work or not is not known for a fact. It is most likely that she wanted him to publish the work because the first script did not include her last poem where she laments the recently beheaded King Charles I. She wrote her elegy hastily probably to include in her book that would be published soon. After she finished writing the poem, she sent it and it was the last poem of her first book. The publishing of her book at that time had a great significance not only for her family's reputation, that had already been disgraced by her sister, Sarah's unusual conduct and heresy, but for the reputation of New England in general. All of her other works were published posthumously.

In 1652 she had her last and eighth child. After Bradstreet had her first grandchild, Elizabeth, in February 1664 from the marriage of her oldest son Samuel with Mercy, the daughter of William Tyng, she became very active in writing poetry. She wrote her best poems during that period. All poems subject of this study are written after that date except for "Flesh and Spirit." The years 1665 and 1666 were full of tragedies for the Bradstreets. First, her dearest grandchild died at the age of one year and a half of some unknown kind of disease. On the death of her grandchild, Elizabeth, she wrote a very touching poem, "In Memory of my Dear Grandchild Elizabeth Bradstreet, who Deceased August, 1665, Being a Year and Half Old." Soon after that, another tragedy struck. On July 10, 1666 Bradstreet's house was engulfed in fire, on this incident she wrote the poem, "Verses upon the Burning of our House." In 1699, Anne the daughter of Mercy, died leaving her family heartbroken. Bradstreet wrote a beautiful and touching elegy, "In Memory of my Dear Grandchild Anne Bradstreet, who deceased June 20, 1699, being Three Years and Seven Months Old" where she mourns the death of her beloved grandchild. Mercy had a son, Simon, who died soon in 1699. Soon after that, Mercy died in 1670 while giving birth to a baby, the infant also died. In the space of five years Bradstreet had to endure the deaths of four of her grandchildren and the death of her daughter-in-law who was so close to her heart as one of her own children.

Anne Bradstreet encountered many hardships in her lifetime; moving constantly from one place to another leaving behind her home and friends, having near-death experiences as a result of illnesses and delivering children, the deaths of her family members including her own children and grandchildren, and to top it all the burning of her house. In all these terrible incidents she found spiritual solace by writing prose and poetry. She was directed to it not only by her talent and character but also by her devotion to her faith. Bradstreet lived the rest of her life in Andover, Massachusetts, until she died in September 16, 1672 at the age of sixty after suffering from a disease that wasted her to skin and bones. During her lifetime she produced a considerable amount of fine literary prose and poetry as one of the most important literary figures in the history of American Literature.

Chapter Two

Bradstreet's Inner Struggle: "The Flesh and the Spirit"

When Anne Bradstreet crossed the Atlantic Ocean with her father, husband, and the rest of her family members on *the Arabella* in a quest for establishing a utopian Puritan colony, they had to struggle for survival. Puritans proclaimed their journey to cross the ocean as a pilgrimage to Jerusalem claiming that they were fulfilling God's command in seeking "the City" (85). According to Harde (63), Calvinism taught Bradstreet that she was, as a woman, worthy of learning and education, just like men, so she would be able to read the scripture; and her time should be spent in "self-scrutiny" in order to better understand and articulate her relationship with God. Bradstreet wrote to her children saying that on arrival to New England: "I found new world and new manners, at which my heart rose" not in rejoice but in disappointment (Ellis 5). She was disappointed for missing her homeland and friends in England and because of the primitive living conditions and the harsh and uncouth manners of the uncivilized people in the New World. She used to live in the luxurious estates of the Earl of Lincolnshire where etiquette and sophisticated manners were taken for granted. Consequently, she believed that God was with them no more, and she questioned their Puritan cause. She continues, "many times hath Satan troubled me concerning the verity of the scriptures, many times by Atheisme how I could know whether there was a God; I never saw any miracles to confirm me, and those which I read of how did I know but they were feigned" (sic) (Ellis 5). Death, starvation, homesickness, and toil were what Bradstreet found in the New World. These were the moments when Bradstreet experienced doubt toward their cause, survival and flourish of Puritan faith. The result was an inner struggle in Bradstreet, arising from the severe conflict between her doubt and faith metaphorically representing the demands of flesh and spirit or good and evil. This inner conflict is a motif that often recurs in Bradstreet's poetry; she even called one of her poems after this inner struggle that she continuously endured: "The Flesh and The Spirit."

Poems that deal with the inner struggle between the materialistic desires and self-righteousness were very common among Puritan poets, such as Edward Taylor, John Donne, Andrew Marvell, Sternhold Hopkins, and many others. For the new settlers, Puritanism was "a spirituality of weaned affections, rooted always in this world but reaching toward the other world" (Hambrick-Stowe 21). "The Flesh and The Spirit" can be described as a meditative poem in the form of argument between flesh and spirit. In an article entitled "Anne Bradstreet" Stanford says that a poet in meditative poetry, after imagining a scene or seeing the subject of meditation, "draws argument from it regarding eternal truths or his own relation to God. The last step is a colloquy with God . . . in which the meditator determines to have more faith, to cease from sin, to abide by God's law, or comes to some moral discernment" (50). This kind of meditation exists in almost all of Bradstreet's poetry. It is one of the devices by which she seeks spiritual solace for the purpose of overcoming any worries that had the potential of disturbing the tranquility and calmness of her soul.

Bradstreet's "The Flesh and the Spirit" was published posthumously in 1678 in the collection *Several Poems*. The subject of this poem is the enslavement of the body to worldly pleasures. "The Flesh and the Spirit" is divided into two parts and is in the form of a dialogue between two personified sisters, Flesh and Spirit. Using the voices of two personified characters is a clever mechanism that enabled Bradstreet to express her doubts in Christian faith objectively. In the first part, Flesh tries to convince Spirit with the importance of the needs of the flesh at the expense of spirituality. In the second part, Spirit defends spirituality claiming that it is the true substance that will grant its follower eternal happiness and salvation. Whether Flesh is correct or Spirit is to be discovered later by investigating each of their respective arguments. The interesting style of dialogue in this poem "enlivens the dry subject matter that Bradstreet wishes to teach" to her readers (Winebrenner, *Puritan Voice* 137). This technique of debating, which is appealing and interesting, was used by medieval poets in didactic poetry comprising the dialogue between vice and virtue. The form of dialogue between divine and profane souls continued to be popular during the 16th and 17th centuries. "The Flesh and the Spirit" runs into one hundred and eight lines of four stressed iambic couplets. Her use of heroic couplet, which was commonly used by Elizabethan poets such as: Sir Philip Sidney, John Milton, and Edmund Spencer, indicates Bradstreet's growth as a mature poet and her consciousness of her poetic merit. Thomas Dudley, Bradstreet's father, encouraged her use of heroic couplet in writing poetry in an obvious attempt of his to make a place for his daughter among other poets. Bradstreet, however, in her more mature and late poems freed herself from the restrictions of heroic couplet and wrote lyrical poems that reflect her beliefs, experiences, and feelings in a more profound and musical way bringing into sharper relief her quest for spiritual relief.

Bradstreet is considered a representative of the ideal Puritan woman. Her poem "The Flesh and the Spirit" is a reflection of the Puritan concept of sin and virtue. This poem, which has many biblical allusions, is in the narrative style. The speaker while standing close to the banks of a torrent of tears hears Flesh and Spirit arguing. The speaker narrates the dialogue between Flesh and Spirit using the first person singular pronoun, *I*. Rosamond Rosenmeier in her book *Anne Bradstreet Revisited* insists on the fact that any interpretation of this poem necessitates the consideration of Bradstreet's use of the first person singular pronoun as placing her or the narrator in the position of a mere reporter or observer (106-7). Hence, the reporter enjoys the detachment from the struggle between Flesh and Spirit; consequently, the reporter may enjoy some kind of credibility. On the other hand, Bradstreet's use of the first person singular pronoun may indicate that this dialogue occurred in the narrator's own mind. Therefore, Bradstreet cannot be considered as simply reporting in sheer objectivity. Both claims can be correct. Bradstreet during her lifetime did experience an inner conflict between her flesh and spirit, as hinted above. In a letter to her children Bradstreet wrote, "as I grew up to be 14 or 15 I found my heart more carnall, and fitting loose from God, vanity and the follyes of youth take hold of me" (sic) (Ellis 4). The reason why Bradstreet uses this technique of merely reporting is to detach herself from the argument between Flesh and Spirit in order to be believable, at least to her readers. According to Stanford, another method of detaching herself from the involvement in the debate between Flesh and Spirit is using the style of argument to express her doubts (85). Then so it happened that Bradstreet got sick and it was during the tiring moments of her sickness that she was able to have recourse to God by restoring her strong faith in God and alienating herself from vice. Nonetheless, like any other thinking person, she too continued experiencing that inner struggle between virtue and vice until the day she passed away. Such an experience is a typical characteristic of a thoughtful mind, duly expressed in her poetry throughout.

Bradstreet describes Flesh and Spirit as two mutually dependent sisters; one cannot exist without the other. Spirit is best presented in comparison to her opposite, Flesh. The example of their mutual inclusiveness and interdependence is to say that if there is no day there would be no night or vice-versa. Therefore, their description as two sisters is very accurate and meaningful. Both Flesh and Spirit coexisted in Bradstreet's person just as they coexist in every other human inner self. Their existence, nevertheless, was inharmonious; hence conflicting.

In most of Bradstreet's poems, the presence of this struggle can be seen, most obviously in all poems subject of this study. "The Flesh and the Spirit" is a tense and self-analytical poem about the conflict between Flesh and Spirit, a conflict that mirrors Bradstreet's own internal conflict between her doubt and faith, her sins and virtues. In the first part, Flesh, whose interest lies in "worldly wealth and vanity" (6), starts the argument with Spirit, "who did rear / Her thought unto a higher sphere" (7-8), by scornful series of questions using "language that suggests a satiric use of scholastic vocabulary" (White, *Anne Bradstreet* 338). Rosenmeier, also, perceives "the bite of sarcasm" in Flesh's questions (*Revisited* 107). Flesh asks spirit why she wastes her life on "shadows which are not" (20); shadows such as: "Mediation" (10), "Contemplation" (11), "Speculation" (13), and "dream of things beyond the Moon?" (15). The very means of spiritual attainment are thus placed here in a poor light as unsubstantial and redundant. Hinting at their uselessness, Flesh continues saying those shadows will not "feed thee," (11) nor will you be able to "dwell" on those allusions (16). Flesh tries to prove that Spirit's beliefs are based on fragile, unfounded logic; and therefore, open to fallacy.

Having decried the goals and means of spiritual attainment, Flesh, then, describes the pleasures of the world as "True substance." These treasures, which spirit considers "sinfull" (57), are "fame" (26), "riches" (29), and worldly "pleasure" (sic) (33). Thus, Bradstreet's pleasures were not "sinfull," and her "riches" were humble in degree, as indicated in the first chapter of this book. Stanford says what is interesting about these temptations of the Flesh is that "they are not expressed as vicious in any way" (86). They can be attained in a sound Puritan manner. It is true that these pleasures can be attained in a sound Puritan manner, but for Spirit indulging in these worldly pleasures will hinder her from contemplating eternal heavenly pleasures; therefore they are sinful, or at least facilitating to sinning. Bradstreet enjoyed the pleasure of being married to a young important man and also enjoyed a reasonable amount of luxury compared to other inhabitants of the New World. Moreover, as a significant poet in the New World Bradstreet was famous for her poetical talent. Most likely, "honour" (25) was more threatening as a sinful pleasure; people surrounding her recognized her talent and predicted that she will have a pioneer name as a literary figure, at least in New England. She was the daughter of the governor, of a learned and prestigious family, the only poet in New England, and the first significant English female poet. However, the sins of "honour" and "immortal fame" (26) may have disturbed her "settled heart" (38). Bradstreet's distinguished worldly status kept her mind troubled of falling a prey to pride. Therefore, she "fought against these manifestations of her 'unregenerate part' with the weapons of her faith; her determination to prevail and her trust that a glorious reward awaited her are expressed in the words in which Spirit continues to admonish and subdue her sister 'Flesh'" (White, *Anne Bradstreet* 340-41).

In "The Flesh and the Spirit" Bradstreet includes many biblical allusions that enhance the charm and grandeur of this poem. Bradstreet employs her knowledge of the Bible not only in this poem but also in other poems, subject of this study. Winbrenner claims that Bradstreet, purposely, rendered Flesh's argument full of "theological flaws" probably to aid Spirit win her battle against Flesh (141). When Flesh, sarcastically, asks Spirit if she has in heaven "treasures there laid up in store?" (17), Bradstreet alludes to Christ's promise in the Bible that is made to his disciples saying that there is "a treasure in the heavens that faileth not" (sic) (Luke 12: 33). The second instance is when Flesh claims that Spirit's aspired treasures are merely "shadows" (20), Bradstreet is alluding to the Christian belief that earth is actually a shadow: "our days on earth as a shadow, and there is none abiding" (1 Chron. 29:15). Bradstreet realizes that her readers will identify with the Christian allusions in "The Flesh and the Spirit"; therefore, the poem's impact on her Christian readers would be more powerful. Bradstreet wishes to teach her readers a moral lesson on how to be able to reconcile with themselves in time of predicaments and be patient believers and fine people.

The second part of "The Flesh and the Spirit" is Spirit's response to Flesh. Spirit interrupts Flesh exclaiming, "Be still, thou unregenerate part" (37). According to Rosenmeier (*Revisited* 107), the phrase "Be still," indicates indirectly that Spirit is "uncomfortable." Harde says that the word "unregenerate," according to *The Oxford English Dictionary*, means fallen spiritually but redeemable (84). According to Puritan belief, all human beings are fallen, just like Flesh is fallen, but not beyond the point of salvation. When Flesh argues that the "True substance" is found in the "variety" of earthly pleasures, Spirit answers back saying that the true substance is found in heavenly pleasures (24). According to Puritans, the true substance is that which is eternal and pleasures of heaven are the only eternal substances. Bradstreet here alludes to the biblical promise that human beings "have in heaven a better and an enduring substance" (Heb. 10:34).

The struggle between Flesh and Spirit is not settled easily. Spirit's exclamation interrupting Flesh's argument, "Be still," indicates how awfully Flesh's argument is persuasive and disturbing to Spirit. Spirit continues, "Disturb no more my setled heart" indicating the difficulty of rejecting Flesh's appealing argument (sic) (38). For Spirit, Flesh's argument is "flatt'ring" and charming (50). Spirit was enchained as Flesh's "slave" (50) until it was able to "stop" her "ears" (55) from hearing the "deadly harms" of Flesh's charm (56). Spirit describes Flesh's argument as appealing and difficult to resist. The same way Bradstreet herself confessed having trouble resisting the temptations of the flesh. Spirit vows to make her twin sister, Flesh, her "foe" (40) until she sees her defeated "in th' dust" (42). Flesh's questions provide points for Spirit to disprove. Spirit, in refuting Flesh's argument, uses the same points used by Flesh in her claims in order to turn the table upon her. Spirit deems Flesh's "True substance," "honour," and "riches" as "sinful pleasures" that she hates because her "greatest honour" (61) and "ambition lyes above" (sic) (60).

Spirit continues her argument with Flesh telling her not to "scoff" (65) the way she lives, for in her words "I have meat thou know'st not of" (66). Spirit's meat, which is "Manna" (67), is "freely given to the regenerate soul" (Rosenmeier, *Revisited* 108). Much of the power of Spirit's argument is the result of the biblical language she correctly employs. Bradstreet's Spirit begins her argument by echoing Christ's statement: "I have meat to eat that ye know not of" (John 4: 32). Christ also tells his disciples: "This is that bread which came down from heaven: not as your fathers did eat manna, and are dead: he that eateth of this bread shall live forever" (John 6: 58). Bradstreet's use of biblical allusions here is to emphasize the righteousness and legitimacy of Spirit's claim. Again, Spirit uses the same points which Flesh uses in her argument. Spirit's "thoughts do yield" her "more content"; they are neither "shadows" nor vain fancies (69-71). Spirit's thoughts yield for "things that are so high" (73). Spirit's pleasures are "Eternal substance" of heaven unlike Flesh's temporary worldly pleasures (75).

The eye of Spirit is able to "pierce the heavens, and see / What is Invisible" to the eye of Flesh (77-78). These heavenly pleasures that Spirit speaks of are invisible to Flesh simply because they are beyond Flesh's "dull Capacity" (74). According to Rosenmeier, Spirit's argument is even more alluring not only because of her use of biblical allusions but also for the fact that Flesh cannot see what Spirit is describing (*Revisited* 110). Spirit does not yield for materialistic possessions such as: "silk," "gold," "Pearls," and "Diamonds;" but for things that are "More glorious than the glist'ring Sun" (82). Spirit aspires for glories that she will "dwell" on in heaven: the City. The following sixteen lines are comprised of the description of "the City," which is a "paraphrase of the description of the city of God in the book of Revelation, that great poetic document which held continual fascination for Anne Bradstreet" (White, *Anne Bradstreet* 341):

> The City where I hope to dwell,
> There's none on Earth can parallel;
> The stately Walls both high and strong,
> Are made of precious *Jasper* stone,
> The Gates of Pearl, both rich and clear,
> And Angels are for Porters there;

> The Streets thereof transparent gold,
> Such as no Eye did e're behold.
> A Crystal River there doth run,
> Which doth proceed from the Lambs Throne:
> Of Life, there are the waters sure,
> Which shall remain forever pure,
> Nor Sun, nor Moon, they have no need
> For glory doth from God proceed.
> No Candle there, nor yet Torch light,
> For there shall be no darksome night. (85-100).

Bradstreet longs for "the City" in heaven, a place made of "Pearl," "Crystal," and "gold." This place where the pleasures are lasting and which has no darkness or gloom because everything with God's grace glows. The poem ends with an assurance of an everlasting happiness for those who were firm in abstaining from the indulgence in licentious desires.

In "The Flesh and the Spirit" Bradstreet "perhaps revealed more of her internal struggle than she realized by making Flesh far more appealing than Spirit" (Durr 214-15). I disagree with Durr here because Bradstreet's Flesh is more appealing though defeated in order to warn her readers that the flesh can be tempting and seductive. Therefore, one should be extra cautious. Rosenmeier notices that Bradstreet is not taking sides with any of the twin sisters (*Revisited* 109). Moreover, Durr's claim that Flesh is more appealing is true simply because she touches upon issues that are logical, tangible, visible, and familiar to humans and therefore more realistic and appealing than the invisible. The human mind tends to believe in what is visible because it exists beyond reasonable doubt; while doubt will always be there, no matter how slight that doubt is, about the true existence of the metaphysical heavenly pleasures that Spirit promises her followers with. It takes a strong faith, such as the strong faith of Bradstreet, to see Spirit's argument as more appealing for it is about things that exist beyond the materialistic world, things that are eternal and not mortal, perceivable though not visible.

Some critics, such as Durr, argue that Spirit's use of the same sensual and mundane terms that she condemns Flesh for using indicates Spirit's hypocrisy (214-15). In other words, how can Spirit denounce Flesh's approval of sensual pleasures while she promises the same sensual pleasures in heaven? Spirit's use of materialistic and sensual terms is very normal and does not imply hypocrisy because these are the terms that are used in every day speech and Bradstreet was only familiar with such worldly terms. Using unfamiliar terms for matters otherworldly and abstract would only add obscurity to the poem. Gordon thinks it is interesting that Spirit "counters each of Flesh's temptations with sensual imagery." Gordon further says that faith is "based on the intangible prospect of a glorious future, and Anne sought to make this heaven a place her reader could imagine" (*Mistress Bradstreet* 269-70). Moreover, desiring pleasures, honor, or riches is not sinful or illicit but living for the only purpose of pursuing and satisfying these worldly desires and ever lusting over them is sinful from the religious viewpoint. Spirit is not merely ascetic; she rejects earthly evanescent pleasures in her preference for heavenly, eternal pleasures. In addition, pleasures in the City are not worldly pleasure simply because they are "transparence" of any riches or pleasures in this world. The paradox of having these sensual pleasures in a holy place like heaven "achieves a remarkable complexity" in "The Flesh and the Spirit (Rosenmeier 110). The sensual pleasures of the flesh are desired by human nature. Couching these worldly pleasures in a heavenly mold make them even more desirable.

Some critics, such as White, have criticized "The Flesh and the Spirit" claiming that the two twin sisters involved in this dialogue represent but "shadowy, faceless forms, glimpsed in the obscurity and gloom of a 'secret place' beside a symbolical river of tears, and what they say to one another is couched in simple language of direct meaning" (*Anne Bradstreet* 342). The poem has drama that exists between "Flesh" and "Spirit" as a result of the reality and intensity of their dispute. Flesh has a persuasive logic to which Spirit offers a tough resistance with her strong faith. Their quarrel is not settled until the end of the poem when she finally rejoices: "I am victor over thee" (62).

Others, such as Stanford, claim that Bradstreet's devotional poems, such as "The Flesh and The Spirit," though "rich in metaphor . . . contain little imagery" (83). The observation regarding simple language, direct meaning, and little imagery in "The Flesh and The Spirit," is however true because the didactic purpose of the poem itself requires it to be direct and clear. Involved expressions and complex ideas could confuse the targeted audience and therefore the purpose of the poem would not be achieved. Bradstreet wrote much of her personal work in order to reconcile herself to God and to work out the doctrines of her faith in everyday life unlike her English contemporary great poet John Milton who wrote his epical masterpiece, *Paradise Lost*, in order to "justify the ways of God to man" (Nichols 53). However, Bradstreet's devotional poems do not lack imagery completely, for instance "The Flesh and The Spirit" has a considerable amount of imagery. Spirit in her answer to Flesh's argument uses the images of a "captive," "meat," and the biblical imagery of "Manna:"

> When I am victor over thee,
> And triumph shall, with laurel head,
> When thou my Captive shalt be led,
> How I do live, thou need'st not scoff, 65

> For I have meat thou know'st not off;
> The hidden Manna I doe eat,
> The word of life it is my meat. (62-68).

Imagery in Bradstreet's didactic poems is mostly less frequent than in her late lyrical poems as will be shown in the next chapter. It is not a result of lacking the wit or imagination for beautiful scenery or witty figure of speech but for the sake of the didactic purpose of this poem.

Ann Stanford says that the core of the argument between the Flesh and the Spirit revolves basically around the Christian belief of the true existence of the afterlife, and secondarily around the worldly pleasures of Flesh, which Spirit considers as obstructions to attaining salvation (88). For Bradstreet, that argument between the twin sisters is an externalization of a deeper inner spiritual struggle with doubt. In Bradstreet's "account of that struggle she relied on revelation through the scriptures and through observation and experience of nature—i.e., faith and reason—to uphold her conclusions" (Stanford 91). Wendy Martin opines that Bradstreet's faith is paradoxically achieved by her hope for heaven which is "an expression of a desire to live forever—a prolongation of earthly joy rather than a renunciation of life's pleasures" (*An American Triptych* 17).

"The Flesh and the Spirit" echoes the battle between good and evil, God and Satan. Satan tries to seduce man to follow his materialistic desires while God "calls on the faithful to accept the afflictions of the body as test of belief in the far greater pleasures of the spirit. The mind and the body . . . [are] . . . arena[s] for the battle between Satan and God," between flesh and spirit (Martin, *An American Triptych* 50). Therefore, the twin sisters cannot co-exist forever, one must eventually prevail. In Bradstreet's case, like it is the case in "The Flesh and the Spirit," spirit always triumphs. Nevertheless, Flesh's argument interspersed with theological flaws paved the road for Spirit to defeat Flesh. This raises the question whether Spirit fairly deserves to win since she simply asserts that she is right and denounces Flesh rather than answering Flesh's questions. Rosenmeier remarks that Bradstreet is not "exclusively" on either side in the argument between the two sisters (*Revisited* 109). Piercy further supports Rosenmeier points of view saying that Bradstreet's dialogue in this poem is "certainly not one-sided argument" (*Revisited* 88). Flesh betrays priority for substances that are tangible, visible yet mortal, while Spirit calls for substances that are celestial, invisible but perpetual. Is it plausible to dismiss these substances as untrue simply because they are unseen for man or do not provide materialistic gain? The answer to this may be debatable. What really matters is believing in something whether it is religion, as in the case of Bradstreet, or home-land, or anything that provides sustainable spiritual joist to its followers. This kind of strong faith will enable its believers to stand aloft in the face of adversity and anguish; consequently, they will be a more productive and successful individuals in their own societies.

"The Flesh and the Spirit" is not merely a "dogmatic poem because Bradstreet honestly and realistically presents the debate between the two sides of man's soul" (Winebrenner, *Puritan Voice* 164). "The subtlety and richness of the poem derives from the fact that the sisters appear to be taking stands neither of which fully represented the ideal. The poem reveals the closeness, indeed the *twinship* of the two points of view, despite the two speakers' declarations of their mutual enmity" (110). Flesh represents that rational side of man that believes in logic and tangible things; while Spirit represents that other side of man that believes in faith and the metaphysical world. Flesh's argument represents the practical and earthly side of man, that materialistic side which Bradstreet had to resist during her life. Flesh's argument appears strong and convincing because it is concerned with visible and tangible things. These worldly pleasures are desired by every human being. Most likely, Bradstreet struggled with her own carnal desires to resist the temptations for earthly pleasures. As a Puritan, Bradstreet could not afford to indulge in such avaricious desires.

Nonetheless, Spirit's battle with Flesh was not an easy one. Flesh always tries to overcome by taking advantage of Spirit's weaknesses. For Bradstreet, her weaknesses were aspiring for "immortal fame," "honour," "Crystal" (93), "Pearl," and "gold" (31). Bradstreet's spirit, like Spirit in the poem, hardly defeated her flesh. Her aim is "high" at the "City" where she can dwell on eternal pleasures (85). Spirit represents the other side of man's mind: the spiritual. Her argument reflects Bradstreet's strong faith and righteousness. Bradstreet's use of biblical language is strongly reminiscent of her method in her poems in which the good of this earth is figured as an emblem or promise of the good to come in heaven. That is how Bradstreet makes Spirit overcome Flesh. However, that does not mean that Flesh should be undermined and denied altogether or "laid in th' dust" (42). Rather Flesh should be redeemed by grace; after all, Flesh is the twin sister of Spirit and the other complementary part of every man's side.

Chapter Three

Bradstreet's Joys and Sorrows: "In Memory of My Dear Grandchild Elizabeth Bradstreet," "Verses upon the Burning of Our House," and "To My Dear and Loving Husband"

In this chapter, three of Bradstreet's poems will be scrutinized in order to explore Bradstreet's search for spiritual solace in times of hardships in addition to identifying her personality as a Puritan individual to reach a better appreciation of her poetry. The study of "In Memory of My Dear Grand Child Elizabeth Bradstreet," "Verses upon the Burning of Our House," and "To My Dear and Loving Husband" will lay bare the secrets behind Bradstreet's resilience in times of hideous familial crises and her affirmative role in society and family as a mother and wife. This chapter will explain how she was able to find spiritual solace during the hardships of the burning of her house, the death of her grandchild, and the long lonely nights when her husband was away on public duty. In the last few years of her life, Bradstreet wrote four elegies lamenting the death of three of her grandchildren and her daughter-in-law. Bradstreet's elegy on her grandchild, Elizabeth, is the best among her late elegies. "In Memory of My Dear Grandchild Elizabeth Bradstreet" is a very lyrical, touching, and smooth poem with beautiful and meaningful instances of picturesque pastoral imagery. "Verses upon the Burning of Our House" is another beautifully composed poem that Bradstreet wrote on the burning of her house in Andover. "To My Dear and Loving Husband" is a private poem that displays sincere love and loyalty to her husband.

The analysis of poems in this chapter is mainly intended to show how Bradstreet was able to accomplish her goals through poetry and resolve her inner conflict between her bodily desires and spiritual goals. It was in the final years of her life that Bradstreet's inner struggle between flesh and spirit reached its climax in her poetry. In "Verses Upon the Burning of Our House," and "In Memory of My Dear Grand Child Elizabeth Bradstreet," Bradstreet represents once again the same argument of "The Flesh and the Spirit" but this time with reference to actual incidents in her life. "To My Dear and Loving Husband" illustrates how Bradstreet was able to find comfort through writing poetry during the long cold nights when her husband used to be away on public duty. Moreover, these poems also demonstrate Bradstreet's deep affection for her family members as well as her important role in New England as a maternal and literary figure.

In the five years from 1665 to 1670 many tragic occurrences struck Anne Bradstreet on the personal level; in 1665 her grandchild Elizabeth died, in 1666 her house burned to the ground, in 1669 two of her grandchildren died, and in 1670 her daughter-in-law died in childbirth and the newly born infant also died shortly after her mother's death. Two tragedies, that moved her to compose "In Memory of My Dear Grandchild Elizabeth Bradstreet" and "Verses upon the Burning of our House," concern the study in this chapter. First, in a hot summer night Bradstreet's most dear grandchild, Elizabeth, died at the age of one year and a half because of some mysterious disease. On the death of her grandchild, Bradstreet wrote "In Memory of My Dear Grandchild Elizabeth Bradstreet, who Deceased August, 1665, Being a Year and Half Old." Soon after that, another tragedy struck, Bradstreet's house in North Andover burned to the ground. In the evening of the 10th of July, 1666 a servant accidentally dropped a lighted candle causing the entire house to go up in flames leaving Bradstreet and her family homeless and without any belongings. In that fire a library of eight hundred books and many personal papers and poems were also burned. On that incident she wrote the poem, "Verses Upon the Burning of Our House." In the space of five years Bradstreet had to endure all these tragedies that generated a kind of a gloomy mood, which stirred her poetical talent to compose some of her finest poetry, through which she was able to find comfort. The poetic statements in the three poems that will be subjected to critical study in this chapter are personal and direct, expressing the intimacy and agonies of domestic life.

Anne Bradstreet wrote several elegies on the deaths of several important figures on both personal and public levels. Earlier in her life she wrote traditional elegies lamenting the deaths of Queen Elizabeth, Sir Philip Sidney, and Du Bartas. Bradstreet, later in her life, wrote more mature and original elegies lamenting the deaths of family members. Bradstreet's late elegies excelled, artistically, elegies by other poets of the 17th century. While Bradstreet's elegies show sincere emotion, expressed in concise eloquent words and in smooth and elegant style, the elegies by her contemporary poets illustrate "impersonal expressions of grief crowded with word play and apologies for the deficiencies of the writer" (Durr 217). Ann Stanford insists on the novelty of Bradstreet's later elegies saying that "Bradstreet's funeral elegies differ from those most often written in New England in several ways. They are without an apology for the writer's lack of skill; they use few and gentle conceits; and the feeling expressed in them is intense and personal" (109). One of Bradstreet's most refined and beautiful poems is her elegy "In Memory of My Dear Grandchild Elizabeth Bradstreet."

Bradstreet's "In Memory of My Dear Grandchild Elizabeth Bradstreet" was published posthumously in 1678 in her collected work *Several Poems*. This self-examining elegy is written at a time of mourning in which Bradstreet expresses profound feelings of love and grief for her deceased grandchild. In this poem, Bradstreet's voice is mature, honest, and original; and her style is smooth, lyrical, and direct. She wrote this poem in two stanzas; in which she used the rhyme scheme of *ababccc*; which, according to Gordon, Bradstreet first invented in one of her best poems "Contemplations" (*Mistress Bradstreet* 274). In this rhyme scheme, which is called quaternion, usually the first four lines pose a question or a statement, and the reply comes in the triplet that follows. The last three lines of each stanza have the same syllabic ending; "the firm, rather somber, Latin-derived "-ate" (White, *Anne Bradstreet* 350). This kind of rhyme scheme puts more emphasis on the triplet, which is the conclusion of each stanza, more than on the previous four lines. Therefore, the focus in this poem stays more on the triplet of each stanza. In her late poems, like in this poem for example, Bradstreet freed herself from the restrictions of the traditional way of writing poetry. She chose to quit using heroic couplets in favor of a more musical and elegant form. Bradstreet was "brokenhearted. She had never lost a grandchild, and in her sorrow, she turned to her old method of managing pain, writing an elegy to baby Elizabeth that combined theology with the intimate, loving language of a grandmother" (Gordon, *Mistress Bradstreet* 274).

Right from the beginning of the first quaternion in the first stanza Bradstreet shows her strong attachment to her grandchild. There are several indications to infer that. What strikes the reader, first of all, is the repetition of the word "Farewell" in the first three lines, indicating her emotional strife to get over the loss of a very dear member of her immediate family. Her deep emotional bond can further be read in her way of addressing her deceased grandchild in terms of affection, such as: "dear babe," "sweet babe," or "the pleasure of mine eye." Bradstreet seems to acknowledge in the first three lines that she had found too much earthly delight in the love of her grandchild, who is no more:

> Farewell dear babe, my heart's too much content,
> Farewell sweet babe, the pleasure of mine eye,
> Farewell fair flower that for a space was lent,
> Then ta'en away unto eternity.

"Farewell" is obviously indicative of separation followed by melancholy for losing that earthly delight (1). The repetition of the word "Farewell" thrice demonstrates how difficult it is for Bradstreet to accept her grandchild's death and how desperate and dejected she must have felt. Some Critics, such as Wolter-Williamson, claim that the repetition of the phrase "farewell" and the phrase "too much" in the first line may indicate irony, anger, and resentment in the poet's tone (179). It is considered an ironical statement because no one can be too much content for the death of his/her grandchild (1). Other critics, such as Piercy, do not see any irony in this phrase and consider the whole poem as a manifestation of Bradstreet's love of God and her grandchild (94). Bradstreet was attached to this earthly object of pleasure, her grandchild. In other words, Bradstreet's heart was too much content with this earthly object of love and delight. Both claims appear to make sense; however, in consideration of Bradstreet's puritan faith and the overall tone of the poem the later seems to be more plausible. It is true that a slight sense of bitterness exists in Bradstreet's tone but that is very acceptable considering the shockingly unexpected death of her grandchild. Moreover, concluding each stanza in this poem by an acceptance and resignation to God's predetermined fate further supports the second claim underlining Bradstreet's protest or disapproval of God's wise judgment. When she describes her deceased grandchild as "the pleasure of mine eye," she emphasizes the love and the human value of her dear grandchild (2). For Bradstreet her grandchild is as valuable as the gift of sight, which is one of the most precious gifts that God has given man.

After grieving over her dead grandchild, who was of deep sentimental value to her, Bradstreet in the third line seems to realize that she has mourned her grandchild enough and grieving more might be anti-Puritan. Winebrenner suggests the same, though sounding a bit harsh, when he says that: "Bradstreet should have known better than to become overly attached to the child" (*Puritan Voice* 183). Therefore, by the end of the first sentence, she moderates the gloomy tone of the poem to a more comforting one. She acknowledges that her grandchild was merely a "fair flower that for a space was lent / Then ta'en away unto eternity" (3-4). The image comparing human life to a flower that is hastily wiped out by God is repeatedly mentioned in the Bible. Bradstreet appears here contently resigned to the belief that Elizabeth, her grandchild, was given to her by God Whose Will it was to take her away. In the poem "Verses Upon the Burning of Our House" Bradstreet clearly expresses that belief:

> I blest his grace that gave and took,
> That laid my goods now in the dust.
> Yea, so it was, and so 'twas just.
> It was his own; it was not mine. (14-17).

Bradstreet conveys her strong faith in God and her trust in the wisdom of divine judgment, saying that all blessings bestowed upon us are from God. And if He, for some wise reason beyond human comprehension, chooses to take that blessing away, she would not protest in resentment. Not only that, but as a matter of fact, she would be thankful for all the other blessings she still possesses.

After that, Bradstreet seems to console herself by saying that her grandchild is now in "eternity," obviously in heaven (4). She continues to console herself thus: "why should I once bewail thy fate, / Or sigh thy days so soon were terminate, / Sith thou art settled in an everlasting state" (5-7). These rhetorical questions imply that the child's departure should be no reason for lamentation since she lives a better life than hers; her life is eternal now while the poet's is mortal. The phrase "so soon" signifies injustice and the word "terminate" suggests cruelty. The irony here is similar to the irony in the first line. Even though Bradstreet tries to be devout and submissive to God; her subconscious betrays her in words that demonstrate the resentment she feels. Having slight feelings of bitterness and anger for the loss of a beloved and innocent grandchild is but natural for an ordinary human being. However, what deserves our notice is her great spiritual strife to get over this unbearable loss by seeking refuge in religiously enjoined patience and submission to the Will of God.

The last line of the first stanza, which sums up the theme in the first stanza, further undercuts any indication of irony or protest that may point to Bradstreet's impiousness; notwithstanding the normal human reactions to such tragedies. She soon disciplines herself into saying no need to grieve any more, for her grandchild is enjoying an "everlasting state" of spiritual well-being. The poem could have ended at the note of Bradstreet's awareness that her grandchild is in an everlasting state of the divine bliss as per the promise of God, but it does not which requires further scrutiny. Wolter-Williamson rightly points out that after her rhetorical question, the poet's grief escalates to anger (180). She answers the question by explaining how she feels instead of explaining how she is obliged to feel. Bradstreet continues her poem to include a second stanza in order to present a more convincing resignation toward the death of her grandchild. Had Bradstreet written only one stanza, her acceptance to her grandchild's death would have seemed easy and unpersuasive. She continues to scrutinize herself on the death of her grandchild and widen the scope to include the subjects of nature and God.

In the elegy on the death of her grandchild Elizabeth, Bradstreet uses pastoral imagery such as "tree," "plums" and "apples," "corn" and "grass" (8-10). White suggests that Bradstreet's use of this pastoral imagery and style may indicate her familiarity with some of Shakespeare's sonnets. But then she continues saying that Bradstreet did not have to read Shakespeare to be familiar with this kind of pastoral imagery since she lived in the wilderness of the New World. As a matter of fact White admires Bradstreet's originality saying that in her elegy to her grandchild, Elizabeth, "heart and hand that mourned . . . were invisible, the grief and trust are clothed in words as old and simple as those that lament the early dead in the *Greek Anthology*, and the poem, a small but faultless work of art, is entirely its author's own" (*Anne Bradstreet* 352). Stanford in her article entitled "Anne Bradstreet," shares the same view with White concerning Bradstreet's "In Memory of My Dear Grand Child Elizabeth Bradstreet." She agrees that Bradstreet having "experienced the actual wilderness" in New England did not need to read Shakespeare's sonnets to produce such a lyrical poem (56). Usually, in the natural cycle things die when they reach maturity. However, that is not always the case. Bradstreet, living in the wilderness of New England, realizes that "plants new set" can "be eradicate / And buds new blown to have so short a date" (12-13). Mawer says that these lines are indicative of Bradstreet's "high, righteous anger" toward God (210). Stanford says that Bradstreet cannot justify the eradication of "buds new blown" and that has caused a kind of conflict and tension in this poem (112). Nevertheless, in the last statement of this poem Bradstreet concludes:

> But plants new set to be eradicate,
> And buds new blown to have so short a date,
> Is by His hand alone that guides nature and fate. (12-14)

According to Winebrenner, "using such a powerful comparison with nature's cycle and the violent word "eradicate," Bradstreet encases her praise to God in irony" (*Puritan Voice* 181). He further says that Bradstreet tries to be a devout Puritan in the last line. However, the "insincerity reflected in the line results from its delayed appearance in the poem. Through irony, she expresses her disapproval of God's ordered plan" (181).

It is true that Bradstreet, definitely, was angry in her capacity of an ordinary human and unable to understand why God would take the life of her precious granddaughter. But as a mature poet and Puritan, she would soon overcome that human frailty and resign to the greater divine plan beyond human comprehension since God eradicates "plants new set," for He alone knows the greater wisdom involved and it is He "alone that guides nature and fate." The last line of the poem, the conclusion, indicates Bradstreet's strong faith and her submission to the divinely ordained fate. The fact that it appears only in the last line does not bespeak any insincerity or deliberate delay mainly for two reasons. First, each stanza is only seven lines and having the conclusion of the poem in the last line of each stanza is not late. Secondly, in this type of rhyme scheme, which is called quaternion, usually the first four lines pose a question or a statement, and the reply or the answer, which is more important, comes in the triplet that follows. Winebrenner seems to forget that this kind of rhyme scheme puts more emphasis on the triplet, which is the conclusion of each stanza, more than the previous four lines. Therefore, the fact that Bradstreet's resignation to the death of her grandchild occurs in the last line does still indicate her sincerity and approval of God's predetermined fate and not otherwise. Stanford, in an article entitled "Anne Bradstreet," supports Bradstreet's use of such form: "The feeling of the strength of grief in this poem, conveyed by so appropriate a form, makes this one of the finest elegies in American literature" (*Puritan Voice* 56).

Death is seen as a part of God's Will. Alluding to the deceased grandchild as "dear babe," "sweet babe," "fair flower," and "Blest babe" in the first five lines, the poem's tone first appears to be cautiously joyful. The tone further promises hope that comfort will ultimately emanate from God's divine plan. The parallelism between nature in Bradstreet's poem and life of Man is significant in the second stanza, because Bradstreet thereby tries to seek order in the chaotic world she finds herself in. A mild strain of protest and tension in the poem can be observed, without which the poem would have lacked the essential human aspect. She is content with the realization that "time brings down what is both strong and tall," since after all, this has been the way of "nature." This belief is engraved on the mind of every Puritan child. Anne Bradstreet used to teach her son, Samuel when he turned three year-old, how to read the lessons of Puritanism:

> *A: In Adam's Fall*
> *We Sinned all.*

And

> *T: Time cuts down all*
> *Both great and small.*

And

> X: Xerxes the great did die
> So must you and I. (165-66) "The New England Primer," in McMichael, *Concise Anthology of American Literature*, (54-44).

However, her protest, significantly just before she concludes her poem, is represented in the word "but." She can understand if an old person dies, "but" she shows unhappiness, mild though in tone and temper, about the death of the "fair flower," "the pleasure of [her] eye," and more importantly her one year-old and a half grandchild. Bradstreet does not imply that God's actions in nature seem to be just while He is unduly harsh towards man. Nor do these lines suggest that the death of a baby is so far outside normal course of events that it inspires outrage. Rather, Bradstreet comes to settle with the belief that God alone is entitled to eradicate new plants, and take the life of her little grandchild in His greater Wisdom. Bradstreet knew "she had no ability to influence the course of events in her life, and so she turned her heart toward God, resolving to stay true to her faith" (Gordon, *Mistress Bradstreet* 274).

Through writing the elegy on her deceased grandchild, Bradstreet was able to find spiritual solace. It is an elegy that has an effect, in Piercy's words, "of lyric delicacy of feeling" (94). Her style is smooth, simple, and direct, which indicates that her feelings are sincere and serene. This ease of her style underscores that her "heart's too much content" (1). She believes that her grandchild is not dead, but rather in "eternity." She addresses her grandchild: "thou art settled in an everlasting state" (7), addressing her grandchild raises the mood of grief to its peak. Moreover, Bradstreet's religion and faith, when received into one's life during this time of grieving, can be a source of guidance and reassurance. She expresses her strong faith and emotions of grief in this poem. However, how strong a human is in his faith, a little bitterness may overcome him/her in the face of tragedies and so a dim shade of resentment is obvious in the second stanza. Kenneth A. Requa says, while writing her elegies for her grandchildren Bradstreet's intention is not to honor the "deceased" but she rather "concerns herself primarily with reconciling . . . herself to the recent death" (*Poetic Voices* 4). The same holds true about Bradstreet's elegy "Verses upon the Burning of Our House," which she penned in order to reconcile herself to the irretrievable loss of her house with all her precious belongings in it including her library. The logic of God is incomprehensible to humans. Bradstreet finds consolation in her realization that God guides the course of nature and fate, and in His wise guidance there is eventually goodness that is not necessarily always apparent to humans, rather it is most often hidden from their eyes. Such realization works for her as a source of inner strength.

Bradstreet wrote "Verses upon the Burning of Our House" in the form of heroic couplet. This poem was published posthumously in *The Works of Anne Bradstreet in Prose and Verse*, edited by John Harvard Ellis (1867). In the burning of Bradstreet's house, she lost all her personal belongings that carried a lot of dear memories. Bradstreet's attachment to these earthly belongings can be observed in the lines of "Verses upon the Burning of Our House;" as an attachment that cannot be interpreted as merely materialistic. The possessions she lost did not only carry beautiful memories for Bradstreet but also allowed her to fulfill a divine commandment, which is entertaining guests. The loss of her house with all what it stood for, evoked Bradstreet's emotions and inspired her poetical talent into writing one of her best poems. "As usual, she comforted herself by scribbling down a poem, this time on a sheet of loose paper that was all she had left" (Gordon, *Mistress Bradstreet* 275). A poem where Bradstreet's inner struggle between her attachment to worldly pleasures and her faith demanding her to transcend it comes up to the surface once again.

"Verses upon the Burning of Our House" introduces a common theme in Bradstreet's poetry: the struggle between flesh and spirit. While the conflict between flesh and spirit in Bradstreet's "The Flesh and the Spirit" takes the form of an intense and visible debate, in "Verses upon the Burning of Our House" the argument between flesh and spirit is rather subtle and implied. While flesh in this poem goads her for the expression of anger, rage, and disappointment for the loss of Bradstreet's worldly possessions, spirit on the other hand calls for fortitude, endurance, and the acceptance of God's wise judgment in the true patience of a faithful believer. This kind of inner struggle between flesh and spirit is something that Puritans always try to maintain in order to continually test their faith, especially in times of predicaments, and hope for achieving spiritual consolation that will grant them salvation eventually. Like many of Bradstreet's poems, "Verses upon the Burning of Our House" carries many biblical allusions and poetical images discussed below.

The opening sentence of "Verses upon the Burning of Our House" alludes to more than the immediate occasion, which is the incident of her house burnt. It introduces the idea of a tired person after a long laborious day yearning for some rest. The opening sentence as well as the whole poem refers to the biblical episode when Babylon is burned to its ruins unexpectedly in a similar manner to the burning of Bradstreet's house. The thundering sound and dreadful view of her house burning in front of her eyes in the first six lines brilliantly bring out the pictorial description of the incident. This description evokes the whole occurrence in the mind of the reader as if he actually is living the experience:

> In silent night when rest I took,
> For sorrow near I did not look,

> I waken'd was with thund'ring noise
> And piteous shrieks of dreadful voice.
> That fearful sound of "fire" and "fire,"
> Let no man know is my Desire.

According to Harde, "The first three couplets involve her physical sensations at the sound and sight of her burning house" (110-11). Her focus particularly on the sense of hearing in these lines is amazing, since recent studies, according to Hubinette, have shown that the sense of hearing is the most powerful of all senses (1). After being awakened, unexpectedly, by the "thundering voice of fire" and the "fearful" cries of "fire," Bradstreet can immediately be seen praying to God: "To straighten me in my Distress / And not to leave me succourless" (9-10). The short description of the fire intensifies the destructive power of the raging flames that brought down and turned to ashes in few minutes the house that the Bradstreets built in months. This rapid pace of the poem creates a horrifying and tense mood. In this moment of horrific catastrophe, with the possibility of getting burned, she remembers her God as the only One that can protect her in the middle of such a disaster. Bradstreet cries to God in this time of distress "not to leave [her] . . . succourless." This cry though is common to those surrounded by a disaster, including staunch atheists and agnostics; here it is not out of sheer distress or desperation but as an echo of inner strength resulting from her spiritual faith.

Once outside, she describes how the flames burned her "dwelling place" (12) to the ground until the sight is unbearable to watch, so in an appropriate Christian response she says:

> And when I could no longer look,
> I blest his grace that gave and took,
> That laid my goods now in the dust.
> Yea, so it was, and so 'twas just.
> It was his own; it was not mine. (13-17)

I disagree with Wolter-Williamson in whose view "the use of the conspicuously descriptive word 'dust' hardly sounds like willing submissiveness or acceptance" (195). Wolter-Williamson's claim might be true only if the word "dust" is taken out of context. In fact, Bradstreet here alludes to the Bible: "All go unto one place; all are of the dust, and all turn to dust again" (Ecc. 3:20). Bradstreet here reminds herself that even the living human will turn to dust, let alone her house built of lifeless materials. It is God's will and therefore there is no need to grieve the destruction of her house. Wilson admires Bradstreet's "Verses upon the Burning of Our House" as "a lovely and deeply touching poem that expresses the trust she had in God in the midst of all His hard providence" (97). Moreover, the whole sentence is a prayer to God thanking Him for all the other blessings He has endowed her with. In the next sentence, Bradstreet exclaims her strong compliance with and acceptance of divinely ordained fate. A little later, Bradstreet inquires why

> . . . I should repine,
> He might of all justly bereft
> But yet sufficient for us left. (18-20)

Although God had just taken away her house and all her belongings, she still remembers the other blessings of God she and her family still retain. This gratitude for God's blessings in spite of the tragedy that has just struck her brings into sharper relief her strong devotion and ungrudging attitude to God.

Winebrenner, however, opines that Bradstreet continues lamenting the loss of her house and her possessions because she does not find the appropriate religious response for consoling. "As a mature poet, Bradstreet truthfully (and artistically) portrays the struggle of the saint on earth and dogmatic responses to that struggle were not satisfying to her, personally and poetically" (*Puritan Voice* 172). Winebrenner maybe correct up to the twentieth line and that is very human-like. The momentum of the tragedy is huge and shockingly distressful to be easily and quickly digested or accepted for Bradstreet, not at this point at least. Hence, while passing by the ruins of her house, she continues lamenting in the hope that she will find spiritual solace at a later stage:

> When by the Ruins oft I past
> My sorrowing eyes aside did cast
> And here and there the places spy
> Where oft I sate and long did lie.
> Here stood that Trunk, and there that chest,
> There lay that store I counted best,
> My pleasant things in ashes lie
> And them behold no more shall I. (21-28)

The wreckage is devastating to the point that Bradstreet's "sorrowing eyes aside did cast" (22). In other words, she could watch no more; it is heart-rending. In this very heartbreaking recounting of Bradstreet's possessions, flesh seems to be taking over. Nevertheless, in the description of her lost possessions Bradstreet does not focus on the lost materialistic possessions, but on the precious memories they represent. Moreover, Bradstreet here alludes, again, to the Bible "He hath cast me into the mire, and I am become like dust and ashes" (Job 30:19). Bradstreet's constant reference to the Bible in almost all of her poems accentuates her strong faith and refutes any suggestions that Bradstreet is in any way blasphemous.

Again, in her description of the lost possessions Bradstreet does not focus on the money value of the lost materialistic possessions, but on their value as means to serve the community around:

> Under the roof no guest shall sit,
> Nor at thy Table eat a bit.
> No pleasant talk shall 'ere be told
> Nor things recounted done of old. (29-32)

Harde's observation in this regard is worth-noting who remarks that in Christianity the rituals of preparing and sharing of meals "link us with the sacredness of life itself, and whoever partakes it becomes a priest. Bradstreet here mourns for the space in which she communed with friends and family, for the things that facilitated that community and her role in that type of sacred experience" (Harde 111). According to him, a fundamental principle in Christianity holds that when a group of people are gathered in Christ's name, he is with them. Bradstreet actually mourns the loss of that saintly privilege of sharing meals and gathering in Christ's name and thus being blessed by his hidden presence.

Bradstreet describes the remnants of what used to be her home, while walking through the debris. She mourns losing the souvenirs of her memories of occasions past and the privilege of entertaining people in the future. She describes her losses in very domestic details emphasizing the difficulty to overcome such an adversity. Bradstreet's house always reverberated with life, joy and prayers; now after it was destroyed by the raging flames, no life she laments will "shine" in it any more nor will the "voices" of prayers and joy will be ever heard. She describes this situation when she says that:

> No Candle 'ere shall shine in Thee,
> Nor bridegroom's voice ere heard shall bee.
> In silence ever shalt thou lie. (sic) (33-35)

Bradstreet in these lines alludes to the Bible where an angel tells John of the destruction of Babylon. In *Revelation* the story of Babylon, a city characterized by its worldliness, mentions God declaring it shall be "utterly burned by fire" (18: 8). Apostrophizing this city, God further promises that once destroyed, "the light of the candle shall shine no more in thee; and the voice of the bridegroom and of the bride shall be heard no more at all in thee" (18: 23). Bradstreet seems to allude directly to these verses when she laments the loss of her household possessions. This allusion allows Bradstreet to turn away from her initial shock and imply how her fondness for her materialistic possessions was faulty, invoking God's disapproval, just the same way as God devastated Babylon for being a city with people given to worldly indulgence and gratification.

As Bradstreet expresses her emotional and physical suffering, the loss of her house where she entertained the community fulfilling a divine commandment, Harde opines, "she revisits Puritan modes of consolation and finds them insufficient. But as she forms a Christology centered on 'him who hath enough to do,' she aligns her overworked and suffering self with Jesus" (112). This devastation and momentary alienation provides her with yet another opportunity to gather herself with even greater force to her spiritual self and realign with God (Christ for Bradstreet). Then, after listing her losses in a touching manner in the second section of "Verse upon the Burning of our House," Bradstreet realizes the inadequacy of her response and begins changing her tone by censuring her feelings of loss as vain and unbecoming of a true believer:

> Adieu, Adieu, All's Vanity.
> Then straight I 'gin my heart to chide:
> And did thy wealth on earth abide,
> Didst fix thy hope on mouldring dust,
> The arm of flesh didst make thy trust?
> Raise up thy thoughts above the sky
> That dunghill mists away may fly. (36-42)

After recounting and pondering on the accident, she concludes her poetic response with a prayer to God asking Him to provide her with the strength that will enable her to endure this calamity. Here Bradstreet no more recollects the pleasant moments her house provided her. Instead, according to Stanford, she chides her heart for lamenting the loss of vanities that would be lost one day anyway, no matter how distant that day appeared to one (108). Winebrenner has rightly noticed that in the concluding lines Bradstreet "recognizes that God's hand can be seen in the burning of her home and that He intended it for her own spiritual gain . . . When the poet has fully understood this she can finish the meditative poem with colloquy or prayer that she was unable to offer earlier" (*Puritan Voice* 174). Bradstreet's line: "The arm of flesh didst make thy trust?" (40) is another direct allusion to the biblical warning: "Cursed be the man that trusteth in man, and maketh flesh his arm, and whose heart departeth the Lord" (Jer. 17: 5).

Turning her eyes away from perishable possessions, she is now focused upon the heavenly home, a resort of eternal joy and everlasting peace. Once she realizes the worthlessness of these materialistic possessions, she hopes for:

> . . . a house on high erect
> Fram'd by that mighty Architect,
> With glory richly furnished
> Stands permanent, though this be fled.
> It's purchased and paid for too
> By him who hath enough to do. (43-48)

Bradstreet becomes conscious of the fact that only in heaven she will enjoy the luxury of staying in a house "with glory richly furnished" (45). That house in heaven is indestructible; neither the raging fire will ever touch it nor will it ever be worn out of time. Moreover, Bradstreet's renewed consciousness that the heavenly house has been "purchased and paid for" by Christ's sacrifice contains additional biblical allusion (47). In the Bible it is mentioned that Christ "hath purchased with his own blood" the salvation of Christians (Acts 20: 28). The spirit behind this stamen is resignation to the Will of God. Bradstreet continues in her humble tone praising God's other blessings and Christ's sacrifice:

> A price so vast as is unknown,
> Yet by his gift is made thine own.
> There's wealth enough; I need no more. (49-51)

Bradstreet does not need her earthly house. In heaven, she believes, there is enough wealth for all mankind, so why should she reject what is everlasting and measureless for what is limited and evanescent? Bradstreet in the last three lines declares that her eyes were fixed on the world above and not on anything here in this world for which she hardly cares:

> Farewell, my pelf; farewell, my store.
> The world no longer let me love;
> My hope and Treasure lies above. (52-54)

Bradstreet does not concern herself with the materialistic world. She aspires for the heavenly world. Naturally, this is a strategy for overcoming the great loss and coping with the resultant hardship.

Furthermore, the poem's power and significance come from Bradstreet's use of biblical language and biblical allusions. This is most clearly seen in the poem's conclusion, where this "realization that she has a better home in heaven is reinforced by her allusions to biblical salvific promise" (Winebrenner, *Puritan Voice* 176). In the last line of this poem Bradstreet alludes to the biblical promise: "a treasure in the heavens that faileth not" (Luke 12: 33). The Puritans based their beliefs and their way of living on the principles drawn upon these biblical anecdotes. These biblical allusions throughout the poem, in addition to Bradstreet's final realization of the biblical promise of unparalleled reward high above, preclude any possibility of irony in the tone of the author. In this respect I find it hard to agree with Winebrenner when he, as I mentioned earlier, says that Bradstreet's long recounting of her possessions is an indication of her failure to find a satisfying spiritual relief.

Wolter-Williamson (196-97) says that Bradstreet in "Verses upon the Burning of our House" uses irony twice. First, Bradstreet emphasizes the loss she feels at the destruction of her home in an ironical tone and then she shifts the focus to praising God. Bradstreet's focus on what God destroys does not necessarily indicate irony. When recounting the loss of her materialistic possessions, Bradstreet is merely trying to find resignation to the catastrophe that has just struck her. Had Bradstreet come upon that resignation readily it would have been an unpersuasive sort of submission to fate. The second instance of irony that Wolter-Williamson points out is, "when she labels her vivid memories of the sharing what went on in her home from dinner to the personal experience of hearing her husband's voice as vanities" (196). Stanford adds to it in a similar strain that "regardless of the rational conclusion, and the reasonable argument that this was all God's property anyway and whatever God does is just, the poem contains a strong feeling of loss not fully compensated by the hope of treasure that lies above" (108-09). Both Stanford and Wolter-Williamson seem to miss the fact that each statement seemingly ironical is followed by a statement that undermines irony in it or is a biblical allusion in itself, as mentioned earlier. Furthermore, in reconsideration of the overall tone of the poem, it is obvious that Bradstreet actually was able to find the spiritual solace she was looking for in time of grief.

For Bradstreet writing "Verses upon the Burning of Our House" was a mechanism to adjust herself with the predicament of losing her house with all what stands for as a home that harbored precious memories or a shelter. This poem is rich in details where Bradstreet "voices her distress at the loss not only of material possessions but also of the respite and fellowship the house and its countenance facilitated. Chastening herself for her attachments to earthly wealth, however, she turns to God for solace and attempts to use the experience as a tool by which she might grow closer to him and anticipate her heavenly home" (Nichols 142). In "Verses upon the Burning of Our House," Bradstreet presents "the conflicting claims of earth and heaven, flesh and spirit" (Winebrenner, *Puritan Voice* 179). Puritans believe that they must avoid earthly pleasures for the sake of attaining the promised heavenly pleasures; Bradstreet presents that belief in her poems in a way that suggests how difficult it is to resist the earthly temptations.

Andy Martin says that Bradstreet recognizes the deaths of mature and old plants or people as understandable; however, the death of a nascent sapling or an infant is difficult to comprehend. She felt like being "cheated by the child's death" (*An American Triptych* 71). As a devout Puritan, Bradstreet believes that God, Who is absolute Goodness, has willed the death of her young grandchild and the burning of her house for some wise reason beyond the ordinary capacity of human understanding. She must simply accept whatever happens as a product of God's will. The slight degree of tension in these poems is not the result of a rebellious Bradstreet blaming God for not allowing Elizabeth to live until maturity or the burning of the Bradstreets house; rather the tension is the result of Bradstreet's limited human understanding that cannot help grieving the loss of her beloved grandchild and her house. In the final lines of both poems, Bradstreet demonstrates humble resignation to divinely ordained fate and this resignation offers the only consolation available to Bradstreet. The elegy on Elizabeth and "Verses upon the Burning of Our House" lay bare that resignation can only be achieved by having faith in the Will of God, despite the fact that man cannot understand that Will.

Another type of Bradstreet's poetry that underscores her pursuit of spiritual comfort is her marriage poems. One of Bradstreet's best marriage poems is "To My Dear and Loving Husband," which is a love poem dedicated to her husband Simon. This poem expresses a great deal of sincere emotion and devotion. It represents the ideal love a Puritan wife should have for her husband, of course in an ideal Puritan marriage. For the Puritans the family is very important, because it is the basic unit that forms a state—the Massachusetts Bay Colony in Bradstreet's case. Therefore, marriage is important and love is essential to a matrimonial alliance. Bradstreet's "To My Dear and Loving Husband" presents rather an unexpected notion, especially to modern readers, about pious Puritan poets in general, and Bradstreet in particular. The stereotypical image of Puritans as being extremely devoted to religion to the point of considering the public expression of legitimate affection to one's spouse as being shameful or some kind of taboo was demolished by Bradstreet's emotional love poems to her husband. Wilson does not see this kind of affection toward Simon Bradstreet who is "a dashing figure. Governor Bradstreet's portrait shows an attractive man with long hair and the glow of good living—not a dour ascetic . . . the popular idea of the typical Puritan" (45). "To My Dear and Loving Husband" is an original and lyrical poem that Bradstreet wrote in search of comfort in the difficult lonely nights when her husband used to be off on public duty.

"To My Dear and Loving Husband" is unique because it touches upon a subject matter that most Puritans of the 17th century would not dare to talk of, at least publically. What further adds to the oddity is the fact that "To My Dear and Loving Husband" is written by a woman in a society that discourages female public activities in general—writing poetry to be more specific. Martin rightly observes that "Bradstreet struggled to write poetry in a society that was hostile to the imagination. Her voice was sometimes subdued by religious concerns; nevertheless, she was able to express the range of her feelings" (*An American Triptych* 9). However, the elite surrounding Anne Bradstreet, people like her father Thomas Dudley, her husband Simon Bradstreet, and Nathaniel Ward, did not share the same male chauvinist ideology as the rest of the society; they were tolerant to women's activities as long as they did not pose any threat to the welfare of their newly established colony. On the contrary, they encouraged and supported her to produce fine poetry. Furthermore, modern readers and critics have received "To My Dear and Loving Husband" and her late poetry very well. These poems are included in many modern American anthologies.

Critics such as Stanford, Gordon, White, Piercy, and many others say that women in New England 17th century were forbidden to participate publically in any kind of intellectual or literary activities or leadership, and scriptural interpretation. Many bring up the example of Bradstreet's sister, Sarah, and Anne Hutchinson to support their claims. Sarah was excommunicated and Hutchinson was banished not because they participated in preaching or public activity but because Hutchinson was creating chaos by insulting all other preachers claiming that the only preacher worth attending was John Cotton. By doing that, Hutchinson created a division in the Massachusetts colony in times where the unity of the colony was counted something sacred and vital. Political leaders in the Massachusetts colony had zero tolerance to anyone who may threaten the unity of the newly established colony. Sarah, on the other hand, was accused of going out of her mind and having different love affairs with men outside marriage. Again, such disturbing and lustful behavior was intolerable in a colony that was established on religious principles. The Puritans were hoping to find a Puritan utopia.

The fact that Bradstreet, a female poet, is the first American poet decries the accusation that all men in New England prohibited woman from writing. Bradstreet's writings were encouraged by a lot of men in New England. In fact, her guide, who shared ideas with her, praised her works, and admired her talent, when she lived in Ipswich, was a man: Nathaniel Ward. Puritan women in the 17th Century "were not supposed to trespass the masculine sphere of literary expression, in reality there was more flexibility and tolerance" (Showalter 5). The case of Ann Hutchinson or the writings of Governor Winthrop about women that they should attend "household affairs and such things belong to women," (67) is the result of living in difficult times trying to build a new strong nation; while men, who are generally stronger physically than women, are given the laborious task such as outdoor hunting, cutting woods, and protecting the colonies from outsiders. During their absence, someone was supposed to stay at home to breed and look after children and take care of the household affairs. Winthrop is not saying that being a housewife is an inferior job, but that only women are biologically and physically capable of giving birth to children, taking care of them, and doing other household chores, which only strong women can survive, for those are very difficult and unbearable tasks.

Bradstreet's family did not consider her marriage poems as being very private or un-Puritan; therefore, they published them. There is nothing to indicate that her marriage poems were not intended for publishing. They carry the same stylistic features as her other poems that were intended for publishing. "To My Dear and Loving Husband" is a lyrical and well-composed poem with poetical prominence. It is one of Bradstreet's most beautiful love poems to her husband. It expresses a profound feeling of sincere affection and devotion to her husband, as all her other marriage poems. The analysis of this poem will serve as a surrogate to explaining all her other marriage poems. Stanford (20) says that Bradstreet's "To my Dear and loving Husband" is close to being a sonnet. It "rhymes in couplets and the syntax is simple and direct." Its beauty is in its simplicity and sincerity. For Bradstreet her husband in her marriage poems is a symbolic representation of peace and comfort she is seeking.

Bradstreet, in most of her poems, uses the Bible as resource to enrich and strengthen her poetry. Moreover, her frequent usage of biblical allusions in her poetry is the result of believing that meaningful spiritual consolation exists in the Bible. Therefore, just right at the beginning of the first line of "To My Dear and Loving Husband" she alludes to the biblical command for spouses to love one another: "a man shall leave his father and mother and be joined to his wife, and the two shall become one . . . Husband, love your wives, as Christ loved the church and gave himself to her." (Eph. 5.25). Loving one's spouse does not come in the way of one's love of God; on the contrary, loving one's spouse is a divine command. Stanford argues that the Puritans believed that "the ideal love finds its consummation and continuation in marriage" only (19). Stanford claims that the common theme in Bradstreet's marriage poems is "the union of husband and wife and the insistence on that unity despite physical separation" (21). Hence, the worldly pleasure and the divine command in this case are consistent. Therefore, the usual tension that is present in some of Bradstreet's poems between the flesh and the spirit is replaced in this poem by strong feelings of love, affection, and loyalty for her husband. And this otherwise worldly relationship emerges as a means to her spiritual gratification.

Bradstreet opens "To My Dear and Loving Husband" with a strong statement informing her husband and readers of the intensity of her feelings towards her husband:

> If ever two were one, then surely we.
> If ever man were lov'd by wife, then thee.
> If ever wife was happy in a man,
> Compare with me, ye women, if you can. (1-4)

The repetition of the phrase "if ever" adds to the musicality of the poem. Critics, such as Rosenmeier, see this repetition in the beginning of the poem as an indication of Bradstreet's feminist ideology. The phrase "if ever two be one," according to Rosenmeier, suggests a union of equals, not only as "spiritual equals but as his corporal one too" (*Revisited* 116). The repetition is an assertion of Bradstreet's intense feeling of love to her husband. When this assertion and celebration of love is followed by a challenge, "Compare with me, ye women, if you can" (4); Bradstreet indulges in the first deadly sin, pride. In her poem "The Flesh and the Spirit" Bradstreet feared drifting away from the path of humility intoxicated by some "immortal fame" (26). In the fourth line of the poem "To My Dear and Loving Husband" she failed to stay self-effacing. Or, maybe it is simply a wakeup call for all women that if they do not enjoy such affection with their husbands, then something must be wrong, especially when considering the fact that loving one's spouse is a divine command. Wolter-Williamson opines that the fourth line forces a pause in the poem that compels the reader to contemplate on the intensity of Bradstreet's passion (136).

In the fifth line Bradstreet continues celebrating her love for her husband using concrete imagery tinged with hyperbole to display the intensity of her emotion for her husband:

> I prize thy love more than whole Mines of gold
> Or all the riches that the East doth hold.
> My love is such that Rivers cannot quench,
> Nor ought but love from thee give recompence. (5-8)

Bradstreet's love of her husband is incomparable not only to whole riches of the earth but to "all the social, cultural, and intellectual riches of the East. By following the doctrinally accepted love for the Puritans, Bradstreet elevates her spouse above earthly possessions" (Wolter-Williamson 136). Keeping in mind that Bradstreet's love for her husband is also love of Christ, the previous lines do not only demonstrate how much she loved her husband but also how much she loved Christ. In the seventh line, Bradstreet makes a more direct allusion to the Song of Solomon when she states: "my love is such that rivers cannot quench," echoing: "Many waters cannot quench love" (8: 7). Her thirst of love for her husband cannot be quenched even by rivers of love. The previous two lines indicate Bradstreet's deep love for her husband Simon. Piercy has rightly observed that Bradstreet's ""To My Dear and Loving Husband" is one of her best known lyrics, an unashamed declaration of their passionate devotion" (84). For Wolter-Williamson, Bradstreet's "use of natural images . . . illustrates her awareness of nature's order. She uses these images in seeking a personal order to her chaotic emotions" (132). Again, in the seventh line Bradstreet stresses the intensity of her love for her husband. Bradstreet's poetry is, like the Bible, full of natural imagery. In fact, many of Bradstreet's poems are replete with biblical allusions and imagery that enrich and refine her poetry.

Bradstreet, then, admits that she finds consolation in her love for her husband during the long lonely nights of winter. Furthermore, she declares that the love of her husband is such a gift as she cannot repay. In other words, she is deeply grateful to her husband for loving her. At the same time, having in mind the Puritan concept established in the first few lines that loving one's spouse is as good as love of Christ, the previous two lines can indicate that Bradstreet during times of loneliness and predicaments seeks peace in her love of Christ. The line where Bradstreet says: "Thy love is such I can no way repay" (9) can be explained in two ways; first, she thanks God for providing her with such invaluable love; secondly, she thanks Christ for his love and sacrifice that saved all Christians from the original sin (needless to say from a Christian point of view). Then, Bradstreet prays that God bestow upon her husband a variety of blessings. In this couplet, a notable change of tone to a more humble one can be seen.

The closing couplet of Bradstreet's "To My Dear and Loving Husband" is a plea to her husband to preserve their love in a characteristically Puritan manner, by loving one another as God commanded: "Then while we live, in love let's so persevere / That when we live no more, we may live ever" (11-12). Winebrenner says that loving one's spouse as God commanded will be rewarded in heaven by eternal salvation (95). Ann Stanford says that the last two lines, had it been written by a non-Puritan poet, would probably be interpreted as either that the couple will have descendants, so they will continue to live on in their line or the couple will be famous as lovers and live on in the fame of their mutual platonic love (25). However, in a sheer Puritan context, which stresses on the divine and graceful love, the last couplet is a plea from Bradstreet to her husband to fulfill the divine command of loving each other so they can continue their love in heaven. If they love one another in this world the way

God commanded them, they would be rewarded by an eternal union and everlasting heavenly love in the afterlife.

Moreover, the closing couplet, Harde says, "teases about the full engagement of the Puritan companionate marriage, and figures their work at marriage as part of grace; such passionate work on earth can lead only to Heaven" (89-90). And in Martin's view Bradstreet "loved life on earth that she committed herself to God in the hope that the joy she felt in this life would be perpetuated eternally in heaven" (*An American Triptych* 7). The same applies to her marriage to Simon whom she adored; she loved him deeply and wished for that love to be perpetuated eventually in heaven, but not letting an immoderate love of the creature supersedes her love of God. For Puritans, the ideal love between a husband and wife may be considered as an analogy to the love between Christians and Jesus Christ.

Wolter-Williamson claims, though erroneously, that the clarification of Bradstreet's love poems to her husband illustrates the depth of her love for husband and "her frustration with God's predetermined plan: it took Simon away on colonial business" (133). Martin says that Bradstreet's poems to her husband, Simon Bradstreet, "make it clear that she loved him deeply" (*An American Triptych* 68). But in my opinion here is no indication in "To My Dear and Loving Husband" of any kind of frustration or anger with God's predetermined destiny. The tone is calm and musical, the pace is smooth, and the images are pleasant. "To My Dear and Loving Husband" is a celebration of love and, at the same time, a plea to her husband to continue loving her so when they die, they will be rewarded with an eternal love in heaven for obeying God's command.

Loving one's spouse is a biblical stipulation; it is not an indication to the attachment to worldly pleasures. Yet, this does not undercut the fact that Bradstreet cherished her husband. In "To My Dear and Loving Husband" the worldly pleasure and the divine command are consistent. What is conjugal love at the worldly level for her becomes her love of God when spiritually elevated; thus, it is two sides of the same coin. Therefore, the inner struggle between flesh and spirit that is seen in some of Bradstreet's poems is substituted in this poem by profound and sincere feelings of love for her husband. Bradstreet's aim when she wrote this poem is to seek spiritual comfort during times when her soul was disturbed by the absence of her husband or by some other untoward incident. She describes her marriage as satisfying, loving, and joyful that is the best of worldly pleasures. Bradstreet's love for her husband not only provides her with worldly pleasures but also fulfills the divine commandment of loving one's spouse. Bradstreet hopes to be rewarded by an eternal marriage in heaven, probably a union with Christ.

The burning of Bradstreet's house, the death of her grandchild, and the long lonely nights when her husband was off on public duty generated an inner struggle in Bradstreet's personality. During these predicaments her inner conflict between flesh and spirit became more intense. The slight feeling of protest that can be seen in some places in poems subject of this chapter is a normal outcome to the loss of a beloved grandchild or a precious possession. However, Bradstreet's acceptance of God's predetermined plan is a sign of her strong faith. Her inner struggle was how to compromise with God's will, which sometimes appeared—at least apparently—unjust towards people, and not to give up on life or protest in anger against God's will. "Poetry writing enabled Bradstreet to endure the conflicts of her middle years when her affections were not sufficiently weaned from her family to permit her to put the demands of God first. Her craft also made it easier to accept the periods of isolation during her husband's frequent and sometimes long absences" (Martin, *An American Triptych* 67-8). According to the Puritan ideology God is all goodness and all just, sometimes His justice manifests itself in ways difficult, if not impossible, for man to comprehend. In her poems, Bradstreet achieves the level of understanding that enabled her to find comfort that this understanding brings. This is accomplished through Bradstreet's use of biblical language in her poetry which bridges the gap between earth and heaven for man and enabled Bradstreet to reach the spiritual solace she has been looking for all her life.

Chapter Four

Life is a Journey: "As Weary Pilgrim"

Anne Bradstreet was on constant move, traveling from one place to another going through different adversities and journeys all her life. She was compelled to take all these journeys going to the unknown in search of Puritan utopia. Just right from the beginning of her life, Bradstreet as a child, in England, had to move from one county to another escaping the harsh and unfair prosecutions the English government practiced on Puritans. Having no other choice, the Puritans had to cross the vast and the furious Atlantic Ocean in a long journey that lasted seventy-seven days at sea exposing themselves to hunger, thirst, drowning, and getting lost in the wide ocean to escape prosecution in England. Anne at the age of sixteen was among them. They were heading to an unexplored and primitive land; therefore, going through many dangers was something expected and most likely. When Anne Bradstreet arrived to the shores of the New World, her journey did not stop; she moved from one town to another experiencing the laborious task of establishing a new town and a new home each time they moved to a new place. She first settled with her family at Salem, then they moved to Charleston, then to New Towne, then to Ipswich, and finally they settled in Andover after a long and tiring wandering of 16 years, where she wrote one of her last poems "As Weary Pilgrim," and died there.

Bradstreet suffered another kind of journeying simultaneously, a spiritual one. She went through doubt and belief back and forth and experienced an inner clash between her flesh and spirit all her life—an inner struggle that is a current motif in almost all her poems. Moreover, in addition to the persistently tiring movement from one distant house to another, Bradstreet had to endure giving birth to eight children, raising them up in such difficult living conditions, the burning of her house, the death of four of her grandchildren, and the long cold nights she spent alone while her husband was away on public duty (as detailed out in the previous chapter). All these tiring journeys both physical and spiritual and sufferings that Bradstreet had to bear made her like a weary pilgrim ready to leave this world. Bradstreet has reached peace with herself for her "body shall in silence sleep / [and her] . . . eyes no more shall weep" (25-26). She expresses her state of mind and her fatigued physical condition at the end of her life in the poem "As Weary Pilgrim."

Bradstreet portrayed herself and her life beautifully by composing "As Weary Pilgrim," which was written on the 31st of August 1669, just three years before her death. It was written in her own hand writing and stayed as a manuscript until mid-nineteenth century when it was first printed in John Harvard Elli's edition of *The Works of Anne Bradstreet in Prose and Verse* (1867), which he calls "Verses; Longing for Heaven, Aug. 31, 1669." After that, in all recent editions of Bradstreet's works the poem is captioned with the first line that is "As Weary Pilgrim." Like many of the seventeenth century poems and many of her poems, "As Weary Pilgrim" is also written in heroic couplet, a style that was popular with most poets around that time. Bradstreet penned her own elegy in such haste that she left it without punctuation. According to Elizabeth Wade White, the "lack of line-end punctuation may be due to the frail and worn condition of the manuscript leaf . . . It may also be explained, along with the unpunctuated date, by the probability that it was written with intense feeling and in haste, at a time when its author was more than usually ill and weak, and did not therefore take the trouble to indicate stops and pauses with her customary care" (*Anne Bradstreet* 355). White's explanation that the poem lacks punctuation due to Bradstreet terrible health and physical conditions when she wrote the poem is more likely because during the last few years of her life she was reduced to mere bones and skin. Recording her death, her son, the Reverend Simon Bradstreet, records in his diary:

> September 16. 1672. My ever honoured & most dear Mother was translated to Heaven. Her death was occasioned by a consumption being wasted to skin & bone & She had an issue made in her arm bee: she was much troubled with rheum, & one of ye women y^t tended herr dressing her arm, s[ai]d shee never saw such an arm in her Life, I, s[ai]d my most dear Mother, but y^t arm shall be Glorious Arm (sic) (White, *Anne Bradstreet* 359).

In his edition of Bradstreet's works, Ellis says that Bradstreet's "spelling and punctuation are carefully followed" (44). Therefore, White's explanation to Bradstreet's lack of punctuation and not careful spelling is very plausible. In other editions of Bradstreet's works the spelling and punctuation of "As Weary Pilgrim" and her other poems were improved.

The poem's "tired couplets describe a longing for eternity and escape from the cares of this world" (Nichols 19). The whole poem is a simile where Bradstreet compares life to a pilgrimage in which the pilgrim is exhausted by the journey he is taking. The pilgrim is now ready to be purified from sins and hopes at the end of his journey to find salvation. The poem is divided into two parts. A closer reading of the poem shows that the first part is a simile in which Bradstreet compares the life of a true Christian to a tired pilgrim who passes through dangers and comes to the end of a long pilgrimage hoping to find salvation. In the second part, which starts at the nineteenth line, Bradstreet, when she uses the first person singular *I*, compares herself to an exhausted pilgrim who has experienced many hardships and afflictions in the journey of life. She is weakened physically and spiritually, and her body aches under the long-lasting pressure of the several journeys she had to take in her life right from childhood until she became a grandmother. This poem reminds the reader of John Bunyan's *The Pilgrim's Progress*. The two works have many resemblances. Both works have many biblical allusions and share the same notion that the pilgrimage's "journey is actually an internal expedition" (Wickers 2). They also employ the same imagery of a weary pilgrim on a journey to seek salvation and spiritual solace.

In the first part of "As Weary Pilgrim," Bradstreet describes true Christians on this earth as mere pilgrims alluding to the biblical verse which says that true Christians are "strangers and pilgrims on earth" (Heb. 11:3). The first six lines clarify the situation of that pilgrim:

> As weary pilgrim, now at rest,
> Hugs with delight his silent nest
> His wasted limbes, now lye full soft
> That myrie steps, have troden oft
> Blesses himself, to think upon
> His dangers past, and travailes done. (1-6)

The tired pilgrim has just finished his long journey and he is ready now to receive absolution. Bradstreet "was tired of weeping and depleted by the 'cares and sorrows' of the last three years. Her body ached. She felt weakened by the hard work of a lifetime, and she no longer was able to cope with the hardships of her existence" (Gordon, *Mistress Bradstreet* 278). The description of the pilgrim's limbs as wasted reminds us of her son's diary in which he reports that his mother before she died was wasted into bones and skin. The weary pilgrim now at rest recalls the hardships, both physical and spiritual, that she grappled with or overcame during her lifetime.

Bradstreet, then, recounts some of the earthly experiences that she encountered on this earth, on the wilderness of the New World:

> The burning sun no more shall heat
> Nor stormy rains on him shall beat.
> The bryars and thorns no more shall scratch,
> Nor hungry wolves at him shall catch
> He erring paths no more shall tread
> Nor wild fruits eat, instead of bread. (7-12)

These earthly experiences will not exist in heaven. Heavenly pleasures are far more delightful than these earthly experiences. The heavenly experiences are lasting and divinely pleasant; they are simply "As eare ne'r heard nor tongue e'er told" (41). These lines carry the same idea as Spirit promotes in her argument with Flesh in Bradstreet's "The Flesh and the Spirit." Spirit says that in heaven there is neither

> ... Sun, nor Moon, they have no need
> For glory doth from God proceed.
> No Candle there, nor yet Torch light,
> For there shall be no darksome night. (97-100)

All these worldly experiences and pastoral imagery of the "burning sun," "stormy rains," "hungry wolves," and "wild fruits" convey Bradstreet's attempt to find order and sense in a chaotic world. Bradstreet continues describing life in the wilderness of the New World:

> for waters cold he doth not long
> for thirst no more shall parch his tongue
> No rugged stones his feet shall gaule
> nor stumps nor rocks cause him to fall
> All cares and feares, he bids farwell
> And meanes in safety now to dwell. (13-18)

In heaven there will be nothing that might spoil the true believer's divine pleasure. For all "cares and feares" will be forever gone (17). In "safety" he will only "dwell" to enjoy the heavenly pleasures by His holy Will (18). God places man in different predicaments during his lifetime to test his faith and only those who survive their tests and prove they have strong faith are worthy of God's grace and salvation.

In the first part of Bradstreet's "As Weary Pilgrim," the different perils that a pilgrim encounters in his journey "subtly echo biblical descriptions of adversity" (Winebrenner, *Puritan Voice* 206). The phrases "myrie steps" (4), "bryars and thorns"(9), and "No rugged stones his feet shall gaule" (15) echo the biblical verses "mirey clay" (Ps. 40: 2), "briar and thorns" (Script. 2: 6), and "gall and travail" (Lam. 3: 5). These call to mind biblical description of earthly adversities and God's promise of salvation for those who suffer from those adversities. Adversities in "As Weary Pilgrim" are those of the body rather than of the soul which indicates that Bradstreet's heart is not troubled by the worldly desires anymore. She prevailed over her flesh. Her images that are couched in biblical terms reinforce Bradstreet's triumph over her flesh. To say that "the weary pilgrim" in this poem "had traveled far" in an indication for Piercy (40) of the several adversities the pilgrim encountered.

The poem shifts in line 19 from a third to a first person speaker: "A pilgrim I, on earth perplext / Wth sinns wth cares and sorrows vext" (19-20). The second part opens with a simile where Bradstreet compares her life's journey to that of a pilgrim's, her own pilgrimage toward heaven. Bradstreet accentuates the similarities between the journey of a pilgrim and her own spiritual growth. Like the pilgrim who encounters adversities in his journey, Bradstreet encountered many perils and predicaments like that of the burning of her house, the death of her grandchildren, and doubting her Christian faith that caused her a constant inner struggle between her flesh and spirit. In all her poems Bradstreet longs for "a better country, that is, a heavenly" country (Heb. 11:16). In almost all of her poetry, Bradstreet emphasizes, repeatedly, this aspiration for a better heavenly country in the afterlife and the detachment from worldly pleasures whether it is a house, valuable possessions, a husband, or a grandchild.

Bradstreet is burdened with the "cares and sorrows" of this worldly life. Man in the earthly life is trapped in the dilemma of sin and suffering. The inevitability of committing sin does not, however, necessitate the surrender to one's flesh. In fact, the persistence of the struggle between one's flesh and spirit is essential, for Puritans, to acquire eventual spiritual solace. Bradstreet's earthly adversities make her stronger in her faith alongside intensifying her yearning for heaven in order to escape the pains of the earth:

> Oh how I long to be at rest
> And soare on high among the blest.
> This body shall in silence sleep
> Mine eyes no more shall ever weep,

> No fainting fits shall me assaile
> Nor grinding paines my body fraile
> Wth cares and fears ne'r cumbred be
> Nor losses know, nor sorrowes see. (23-30)

Now, Bradstreet longs for the release, which death will bring, from the limitations and weariness of her body. Death, which represents for her rest and peace, is the only way to be united with Christ. Death will elevate her from this earthly place to a heavenly one where she will not weep, fear, or care anymore. Nichols says that Bradstreet is tired of the physical limitation of her body, the suffering and misery, and the loss of her family members. She hopes for "resurrection and eternity spent with Christ" (19). The previous lines are genuine expressions "of world-weariness and the details clearly convince the reader of Bradstreet's sincere longing for heaven" (Winebrenner, *Puritan Voice* 210). In heaven, Bradstreet will never suffer the loss of a house, a beloved one, or the pain of illness. In this poem "there is no poverty and illness; everything is clean, orderly, and beautiful. The lines reflect a place far removed from the chaos of Bradstreet's earthly existence challenged by illness, fear, and the inevitable sentence of death" (Wolter-Williamson 170).

At the end of "As Weary Pilgrim" Bradstreet uses the image of "Bridegroom," which, according to Rosenmeier (*Revisited* 120), is an indication of Bradstreet's wish for "sexual reunion," although there is "no mention of the literal husband . . . Instead the language is directed to Christ as a bridegroom." Therefore, I do not think that Bradstreet in this poem is aspiring for "sexual reunion" in the literal sense because she knows for a fact that the heavenly pleasures after she dies transcend any earthly pleasure man has ever known. Bradstreet is simply aspiring for union with God—Christ in her faith. Winebrenner sees Bradstreet's use of the images "corrupt carcass" and "Bridegroom," as indications that "convey her faith in God's promise of salvation," which makes it possible for Bradstreet to resist the temptation and seduction of the flesh (Winebrenner, *Puritan Voice* 211).

> And when a few yeares shall be gone
> This mortal shall be cloth'd upon
> A Corrupt Carcasse downe it lyes,
> a glorious body it shall rise
> In weakness and dishonour sowne
> in power 'tis rais'd by Christ alone
> Then soul and body shall unite
> and of their Maker have the sight
> Such lasting joys shall there behold

> As eare ne'r heard nor tongue e'er told
> Lord make me ready for that day,
> then Come deare bridgrome Come away. (33-44)

Bradstreet relishes the thought of all the sufferings she would leave behind in death. She aspires for the freedom from her "mortal" and "corrupt" corpse. Thanatos is what weighs heavily on her mind at the moment; that freedom can only be attained by death. Bradstreet's mood in these lines is gloomy over delay in the approach of death, her door to eternity, while she despises her body in words such as: "mortal," "Corrupt Carcasse," and "In weakness and dishonour sown" (34-37). Then, she states clearly her hope to unite with Christ and thus have a glimpse of God. Bradstreet knows that being "among the blest" is a bliss and eternal joy that is beyond imagination. She ends this poem by begging God to take her into His arms and allow her to "behold" the "lasting joys" of His love, crying, "Lord make me ready for that day / then Come deare bridgrome Come away." "Bradstreet's argument turns . . . on a refusal to negate the body entirely . . . Bradstreet concludes by returning to the bridegroom whose loss she mourned in the verses on the burning of her house" (Winebrenner, *Puritan Voice* 114). Again, similar to the notion expressed in the elegies to her grandchildren, death for Bradstreet seems a comforting idea.

Puritans "accept struggle as an essential part of their lives as pilgrims or pioneers" (Martin, *An American Triptych* 7). In "As Weary Pilgrim" Bradstreet ends the lifelong self-scrutiny and her inner struggle between flesh and spirit. She comes in term of peace with her soul. Piercy notices that "at last, as she came to the end of her journey, doubts had vanished and her faith was secure" (40). Seduction, skepticism, and carnal temptation of the flesh do not threaten her faith anymore. Therefore, the tension that exists in most of Bradstreet's poetry as a result of this inner conflict does not exist in "As Weary Pilgrim." This poem of "valediction seems to go far back in time for spiritual origins and for the stark simplicity of the imagery with which the author expresses her acceptance of life's laborious journey and her expectation of immortality" (White, *Anne Bradstreet* 345). Bradstreet in this poem alludes to 1 Corinthians in the Bible, which compares man's resurrection to her won resurrection to be united with Christ:

> So also is the resurrection of the dead.
> It is sown in corruption; it is raised in incorruption.
> It is sown in dishonour; it is raised in
> glory: it is sown in weakness; it is raised in power. (15: 42-43)

Bradstreet ends the poem by extending her reference to Christ in the concluding couplet: "Lord make me ready for that day, / Then come, dear

Bridegroom, come away" (43-44). This biblical reference to the Bridegroom is mentioned in more than one place in Bradstreet's poems. It alludes to the Bridegroom of the Song of Solomon and her earlier description of her grave as a bed is now extended and suggests that her grave is a marriage bed with Christ, her bridegroom, prepared for her in heaven after she is resurrected.

In "As Weary Pilgrim," the flesh prepares the body for its final rest while the spirit aspires for union with God or Christ in heaven, to use her terminology. Unlike all her previous poems, the tone in "As Weary Pilgrim" is fully assured of grace throughout. The tension, inner struggle between virtue and evil, doubt, and the suffering of loss do not exist anymore. Bradstreet advocates that the spirit will ascend and the physical weariness will go away if man purges his soul of the burden of the bodily desires. However, for Bradstreet flesh's consumption happens in "the bed Christ did perfume" (32). "The loving and sensual connection of the suffering body to Christ's earthly body gives way to glorification of the mortal body through bodily resurrection" (Winebrenner, *Puritan Voice* 113). Stanford also says that the second part is a "resurrection to come," in the form of a "wedding song" that is "adapted to represent the union of Christ with his church or with the human soul" (116). For Bradstreet union with Christ represents her ultimate dream that will grant her salvation and heaven, eventually. This hope for union with Christ is also a current motif in her later poems in particular.

The irony in "As Weary Pilgrim," according to Wolter-Williamson, is in showing the predicaments the true Christian or the pilgrim is put on in God's ordained plan. Similarly, Wolter-Williamson continues saying that even though Bradstreet sacrifices "this fleshly world, ironically, she remains tied to it until God randomly decides to retrieve her to His order" (199). Concerning the dilemma of the true Christian it cannot simply be called irony because God has placed man in such a predicament to test his faith, only true believers can survive trials and tribulations of worldly life. Those who survive are only worthy of God's grace and heaven. Regarding the second ironical point that Wolter-Williamson raises, as explained in the third chapter, God the omnipotent who is absolute goodness and wisdom in ways that are beyond the limited capacity of human understanding does not "randomly" or purposelessly act in the universe. God ordains everything in this world for some wise purpose that man cannot comprehend.

In "As Weary Pilgrim," Bradstreet's inner struggle between her flesh and spirit comes to an end. The pleasures and agonies of life no more count. Bradstreet now is concerned with contemplation on afterlife. Bradstreet's inner conflict is finally resolved. Bradstreet had her "doubts about salvation and eternal life for much of her life" (Martin, *An American Triptych* 21). She had her moments of doubt during times of predicaments, and that is very human-like, but she never disbelieved the reality of salvation or eternal life. According to Martin (*An American Triptych* 53), Thomas Hooker and Thomas Shepard say that redemption is blessing from God, the most merciful and most graceful, bestowed upon those who are considered true believers. Therefore, continual self-scrutiny and introspection are necessary in order to have a heart prepared to be called by God to be united with Him. For Puritans, misfortune and afflictions are to be welcomed as part of God's chastisement. Therefore, the tension that usually exists in Bradstreet's poetry is replaced here by a serene and reassured tone that is certain of its final refuge. In "As Weary Pilgrim" Bradstreet finally finds the spiritual solace she has been seeking all of her life. She discovers that relief from life's burdens comes only after death. Her strong faith and her talent in writing poetry helped her find the peace she has been seeking all of her life.

Conclusion

Anne Bradstreet, the first American poet, encountered in her lifetime many hardships and predicaments. She suffered the English prosecutions and discrimination practiced on Puritans. Then, she had to leave her homeland, to save her life, to the an unknown and uncultivated New World. In the New World, she had to live in difficult living conditions, undergoing sickness and pangs of childbirth, the burning of her house, and the death of four of her grandchildren. All of these adversities caused her not only an agonized mind but also a traumatized soul resulting in an internal struggle. Through writing poetry, in which she meditated on the eternal truth and prayed to God for comfort using many biblical allusions and images, she was able to find spiritual solace. Her strong faith and resilience enabled her to find spiritual comfort and to overcome the adversities she encountered in her life believing she will be rewarded in the afterlife. Bradstreet presented herself in her poems as a fine wife, mother, and literary figure (a model to look up to not only by her own sex but rather by both sexes) as a good and productive individual who contributed tremendously to building her community in all aspects of life. Her poetical talent tops the greatest Puritan poet of her lifetime, Edward Taylor. When comparing them, according to Rich, Bradstreet's "voice is direct and touching, rather than electrifying in its tensions or highly coloured in its values" (Rich xix).

This examination of Bradstreet's poetry is aimed at achieving a more intensive understanding and appreciation of her work, character, and ideology. It also discloses the secrets of her life that enabled her to stand aloft in facing the predicaments she had to encounter. Moreover, the study of her poetry brings into sharper focus the essence of the Puritan ideology, Bradstreet's own faith. Bradstreet shows forth as an example of strong faith; despite the hardships and miseries she suffered, she accepts her destiny without a serious grumble. However, that acceptance is not attained easily. Bradstreet, as demonstrated in the poems of this study, goes through a serious internal conflict between faith and doubt, spirit and flesh, God and Satan. Thus, she presents herself as an example of a fine, honorable, and diligent individual in New England firmly rooted in religiously inspired patience and fortitude. Writing poetry, with such a strong faith in God, enabled her to defeat all adversities believing that after each storm comes calm. More importantly, she believes God will reward her patience with a better and eternal heavenly life after she dies.

Her inner conflict between faith and doubt is best presented in a poem that she names after her own internal struggle, "The Flesh and the Spirit." The argument in this poem between Flesh and Spirit echoes not only Bradstreet's struggle between vice and virtue but rather echoes the struggle of every human being on earth seeking to find spiritual solace. Bradstreet in this poem not only presents the answer for comforting one's self but also conveys to her readers what kind of reward will be granted to those who suppress their sinful carnal desires in order to obtain God's grace. In an answer to Wolter-Williamson's remark, who says that man in this life is trapped in an ironical dilemma. Wolter-Williamson's claims that one "must live in a fallible world with a fallible sense of sin and yet avoid sin" (173). It is true that avoiding sin completely is almost impossible, Bradstreet confessed in a letter to her children that she could not resist sin: "as I grew up to be 14 or 15 I found my heart more carnall, and fitting loose from God, vanity and the follyes of youth take hold of me" (Ellis 4). Therefore, life can be agonizing for all human beings whether they are true believers, like Bradstreet, or not. However, Bradstreet's answer to this dilemma is that only those who try their level best to abstain from sin as much as possible and endure God's tests deserve to be rewarded. Bradstreet tolerates all hardships that she suffered in her life in the hope that she will be rewarded in heaven. Thus, the puritan in her seems to stress that only those who endure the earthly hardships and resist the temptation of the flesh shall ultimately be rewarded with heavenly bliss. After all, no pain no gain.

In other poems, such as "In Memory of My Dear Grand Child Elizabeth Bradstreet" and "Verses upon the Burning of Our House," Bradstreet deals with the issue of loss and acceptance of the divinely ordained fate. In both poems Bradstreet suffers losing something very dear to her heart; she mourns the loss of her beloved grandchild in the first poem and the loss of her house with all her personal belongings in the second. During this time of grief, Bradstreet's inner clash between flesh and spirit is intensified. In both poems, she responds to both catastrophes in a sane and proper Puritan manner. She expresses her sorrow and bitterness in a moderate and acceptable tone without offending God's omnipotence. She, optimistically and gratefully, acknowledges God's other blessings and wisdom in her tragedies believing that some great goodness will emerge from her calamity. In the case of the death of her grandchild,

Bradstreet believes that her grandchild is in a better everlasting bliss with God and she hopes that she will join her grandchild in that unity with God when she dies. In the incident of her house being engulfed in flames, she aspires that God will compensate her earthly loss with a heavenly house. In her meditative poems "and her poems of resignation it is precisely her trust in an everlasting union with God that enables her to bear whatever has happened. Anne Bradstreet's poetry is pervaded by the spirit of a loving God whose mysterious ways work only unto good" (Laughlin 16).

Bradstreet's "To My Dear and Loving Husband" is a love poem dedicated to her husband, Simon Bradstreet. She wrote this poem to celebrate their matrimonial love and comfort herself during Simon's absence. Rosamond Rosenmeier, in an article entitled "'Divine Translation': A Contribution to the Study of Anne Bradstreet's Method in the Marriage of Poems," says that the "prospect of salvation seems to have been evoked most vividly for Anne Bradstreet in her later years in poems about her marriage . . . she portrays herself as passionate, sometimes anxious, but more often as sure of herself in the marriage relationship" (129). Bradstreet does not present herself as a stereotypical submissive wife. Moreover, her love for her husband is not merely a worldly love; it is rather a submission to a divine command for spouses to love each other. Their union in their marriage bond is a vehicle to a more holy, supreme, and eternal union with Christ. The fact that Bradstreet dedicated five passionate marriage poems to her husband belies any indication of irony on her part in any of her marriage poems.

"As Weary Pilgrim" is Bradstreet's own elegy in which she finally comes to peace with her soul. The constant inner struggle between Bradstreet's flesh and spirit that she suffered and maintained throughout her lifetime comes to an end three years before she dies. Bradstreet, as a devout Puritan, has been continuously testing her faith in order to polish it. Three years before her death, she is ready to leave this world. Her worldly desires do not disturb or tempt her anymore; her spirit defeats her flesh. In this poem as in most of her later poems, she uses the Bible as a resource to enrich and strengthen her poetry. Moreover, her frequent use of biblical allusions in her poetry is the result of believing that salvation exists in the word of God which for her is the Bible. Insertion of these biblical allusions in her poetry has a powerful impact on her readers, especially Christians, for their prominence at both figurative and stylistic levels. Bradstreet wishes to share with her readers a spiritual experience about how to be able to reconcile with themselves in time of predicaments through spiritual fortitude.

Bradstreet, like any pious Puritan, realizes that this world is mortal and bound to perish; here lies the crisis of the Puritan spirituality. People are doomed to suffer the loss of their loved ones and things; it is an inevitable outcome of living in this fallible world. Virtuous deeds, for Bradstreet and Puritans, sparked by anguish became a means for a deeper sanctification. They still did not abandon the things of this world but humbly offered them up to the transcendent God. This pious lifestyle presented the Puritans in this world as strange travelers and pilgrims. Anne Bradstreet, the weary pilgrim, encountered many hardships and adversities in her lifetime. In all these terrible incidents she found spiritual solace in writing prose and poetry. She was directed to it not only by her talent and character but also by her faith. Poetry writing for her was a kind of spiritual exercise, where she expresses the thoughts of her soul, confesses her doubts, announces her earthly desires, and declares her aspiration for spiritual growth. Bradstreet, during her lifetime, produced a considerable amount of fine literary prose and poetry as the first significant English female poet and the first North American poet and left behind a name not to be ignored.

BIBLIOGRAPHY

Allen, Gay Wilson; Walter B. Rideout, and James K. Robinson, eds. *American Poetry*. NY: Harper & Row, 1965.

Amore, Adelaide P. *A Woman's Inner World: Selected Poetry and Prose of Anne Bradstreet*. Lanham, NY: UP of America, 1982.

Arner, Robert D. "The Structure of Anne Bradstreet's Tenth Muse." *Discoveries & Considerations: Essays on Early American Literature & Aesthetics Presented to Harold Jantz*. Ed. Calvin Israel. Albany, NY: State University of New York Press, 1976. 46-66.

Blackstock, Carrie Galloway. "Anne Bradstreet and Performativity: Self-Cultivation, Self-Deployment." *Early American Literature*. 32.3 (1997): 222-48.

Borrelli, Jane R. *"Now in an Huddling Croud I'm All Alone": Voice in American Elegies*. Diss. State University of New York at Albany, 1991. *Dissertations & Theses: Full Text*. ProQuest. Albany, NY. 22 Jan. 2009 <*http://www.proquest.com/*> PDF file.

Boschman, Robert. *In The Way of Nature: Ecology and Westward Expansion in the poetry of Anne Bradstreet, Elizabeth Bishop and Amy Calmpitt*. Jefferson, NC: McFarland, 2009.

Brackett, Virginia. "The Countess of Lincoln's Nurseries as Inspiration for Anne Bradstreet." *Notes and Queries* 42.240 (1995): 364-66.

—. "Putting the Flowers in." *Arachne: An Interdisciplinary Journal of the Humanities* 7.1-2 (2000): 5-20.

Bradford, William. "From Of Plymouth Plantation." *Anthology of American Literature. Colonial Through Romantic*. 2nd ed. Vol. 1. Ed. George McMichael. NY: Macmillan, 1980. 31-44.

Brandt, Ellen B. "Anne Bradstreet: The Erotic Component in Puritan Poetry." *Women's Studies*. 7.1-2 (1980): 39-53.

Bush, Douglas. *The English Literature in Earlier Seventeenth Century 1600-1660*. 2nd ed. Eds. F. P. Wilson & Bonamy Dobree. London: Oxford UP, 1962.

Caldwell, Patricia. "Why Our First Poet Was a Woman: Bradstreet and the Birth of an American Poetic Voice." *Prospects: An Annual Journal of American Cultural Studies*. 13 (1988): 1-35.

Caldwell, Luther. ed. *An Account of Bradstreet, the Puritan Poetess, and Kindred Topics*. Lynn, MA: Nicholes P, 1898.

Cogliano, Dan. Publisher of PDF. *The King James Version of the Holy Bible*. March, 2001. Retrived electronically 10 Nov. 2009. <*www.davince.com/bible*> PDF file.

Cowell, Pattie and Ann Stanford, eds. *Critical Essays on Anne Bradstreet*. Boston: Hall, 1983.

Craig, Raymond A. "Singing with Grace: Allusive Strategies in Anne Bradstreet's 'New Psalms'." *Studies in Puritan American Spirituality*. 1 (1990): 148-69.

Cuddon, J. A. ed. *The Penguin Dictionary of Literary Terms and Literary Theory*. 3rd ed. London: Penguin, 1992.

Daly, Robert. "Powers of Humility and the Presence of Readers in Anne Bradstreet and Phillis Wheatley." *Studies in Puritan American Spirituality*. 4 (1993): 1-24.

Derounian-Stodola, Kathryn Zabelle. "'The Excellency of the Inferior Sex': The Commendatory Writings on Anne Bradstreet." *Studies in Puritan American Spirituality*. 1 (1990): 129-47.

Dolle, Raymond. *Anne Bradstreet: A Reference Guide*. MA: Hall & Co. Boston, 1990.

Doriani, Beth M. "'Then Have I . . . Said With David': Anne Bradstreet's Andover Manuscript Poems and the Influences of the Psalm Tradition." *Early American Literature* 24.1 (1989): 52-69.

Durr, Jimmie Cardl Still. *Anne Bradstreet in the Tradition of English Women Writers*. Diss. The University of Mississippi, 1978. *Dissertations & Theses: Full Text*. ProQuest. Tuscaloosa, MS. 22 Jan. 2009 <*http://www.proquest.com/*> PDF file.

Eaton, Sara. "Anne Bradstreet's 'Personal' Protestant Poetics." *Women's Writing* 4.1 (1997): 57-71.

Eberwein, Jane Donahue, Ed. *Early American Poetry, Selected from: Bradstreet, Taylor, Dwight, Freneau, and Bryant*. Madison, WI: Wisconsin UP, 1978.

—. "Anne Bradstreet (c.1612-1672)." *Legacy: A Journal of American Women Writers* 11.2 (1994): 161-69.

—. "'Art, Natures Ape': The Challenge to the Puritan Poet." *Poetics in the Poem: Critical Essays on American Self-Reflexive Poetry*. Ed. Dorothy Z.

American University Studies IV (EL&L). Series No: 184. NY: Peter Lang, 1997. 24-45.

Engberg, Kathrynn Grace Seidler *The Right to Write: Anne Bradstreet and Phillis Wheatley.* Diss. The University of Alabama, 2006. *Dissertations & Theses: Full Text.* ProQuest. Tuscaloosa, AL. 22 Jan. 2009 <http://www.proquest.com/>

Elliot, Emory. "The Development of the Puritan Funeral Sermon and Elegy." *Early American Literature.* 15 (1980): 151-61.

Ellis, John Harvard, ed. *The Work of Anne Bradstreet in Prose and Verse.* Charlestown, MA: Abram Cutter, 1867. Retrieved 22 Jan. 2009. by <http://books.google.com/> PDF file.

Eur, Do-seon. "Reading Anne Bradstreet's 'Contemplations' in the Light of the Emblematic Structure." *Literary Calvinism and Nineteenth-Century American Women Authors.* Ed. Michael Schuldiner. *Studies in Puritan American Spirituality.* Lewiston, NY: Mellen, 1997. 45-69.

Ferszt, Elizabeth *Rejecting a New English Aesthetic: The Early Poems of Anne Bradstreet.* Diss. Wayne State University, 2006. *Dissertations & Theses: Full Text.* ProQuest. MI, Wayne. 22 Jan. 2009 <http://www.proquest.com/> PDF file.

Fischer, Avery R. "Bradstreet's 'On My Dear Grandchild Simon Bradstreet and 'Before the Birth of One of Her Children.'" *Explicator* 59.1 (2000): 11-14.

Gamble, Sandra Craig *Anne Bradstreet: The Sacred and the Profane.* Diss. Lehigh University, 1998. *Dissertations & Theses: Full Text.* ProQuest. Bethlehem, PA. 22 Jan. 2009 <http://www.proquest.com/> PDF file.

Garcia-Rouphail, Maria. *Anne Bradstreet, Her Poetry, and the Policies of Exclusion: a Study of the Developing Sense of Poetic Purpose.* Diss. The Ohio State University, 1982. *Dissertations & Theses: Full Text.* ProQuest. Columbus, OH. 22 Jan. 2009 <http://www.proquest.com/> PDF file.

Gillespie, Katharine. "'This Briny Ocean Will O'erflow Your Shore': Anne Bradstreet's 'Second World' Atlanticism and National Narratives of Literary History." *Symbiosis: A Journal of Anglo-American Literary Relations* 3.2 (1999): 99-118.

Gordon, Charlotte Conover. *Incarnate geography: Toward an American poetics. Anne Bradstreet's Discovery of a New World of Words in Seventeenth Century New England.* Diss. Boston University, 2001. *Dissertations & Theses: Full Text.* ProQuest. Boston, MA. 22 Jan. 2009 <http://www.proquest.com/> PDF file.

—. *Mistress Bradstreet: The Untold Life of America's First Poet.* NY: Little, Brown & Company, 2005.

Hambrick-Stowe, Charles. ed. *Sources of American Spirituality: Early New England Meditative Poetry Anne Bradstreet and Edward Taylor.* Mahwah, NJ: Paulist P, 1988.

Hammond, Jeffrey A. "'Make Use of What I Leave in Love': Anne Bradstreet's Didactic Self." *Religion and Literature* 17.3 (1985): 11-26.

—. "The Puritan Elegiac Ritual: From Sinful Silence to Apostolic Voice." *Studies in Puritan American Spirituality* 2 (1991): 77-106.

Harde, Roxanne *"Where My Hands Are Cut, Her Fingers Will Be Found Inside—": American Women's Writing and the Tradition of Feminist Theology.* Diss., 2003. *Dissertations & Theses: Full Text.* ProQuest. Kingston, ON, Can. 22 Jan. 2009 <http://www.proquest.com/> PDF file.

Harvey, Tamara. "'Now Sisters . . . Impart Your Usefulness and Force': Anne Bradstreet's Feminist Functionalism in the Tenth Muse (1650)." *Early American Literature* 35.1 (2000): 5-28.

Hensley, Jeannine. "Anne Bradstreet's Wreath of Thyme." *Major Writers of Early American Literature.* Ed. Everett Emerson. Madison: Belknap, 1972. xxi-xxxv.

Hubinette, John. "Music and Sound Effects in Horror Films." <http://www.eng.umu.se/monster/john/sound_music.htm> Oct., 2009.

Irvin, William J. "Allegory and Typology 'Imbrace and Greet': Anne Bradstreet's 'Contemplations.'" *Early American Literature* 10 (1975): 30-46.

Ivic, Christopher. "'Our British Land': Anne Bradstreet's Atlantic Perspective." *Archipelagic Identities: Literature and Identity in the Atlantic Archipelago, 1550-1800.* Eds. Philip Schwyzer and Simon Mealor: Aldershot, Eng.: Pagination, 2003. 195-204.

Jed, Stephanie. "The Tenth Muse: Gender, Rationality, and the Marketing of Knowledge." *Women, 'Race,' and Writing in the Early Modern Period.* Eds. Margo Hendricks and Patricia Parker. London: Routledge, 1994. 195-208.

Kehler, Dorothea. "Anne Bradstreet and Spenser." *American Notes and Queries* 8 (1970): 135.

King, Anne. "Anne Hutchinson and Anne Bradstreet: Literature and Experience, Faith and Works in Massachusetts Bay Colony." *International Journal of Women's Studies* 1 (1978): 445-67.

Kopacz, Paula. "'Men Can Do Best, and Women Know It Well': Anne Bradstreet and Feminist Aesthetics." *Kentucky Philological Review* 2 (1987): 21-29.

—. "'To finish what's begun': Anne Bradstreet's Last Words." *Early American Literature.* 23.2 (1988): 175-187.

Latta, Kimberly. "'Such Is My Bond': Maternity and Economy in Anne Bradstreet's Writing." *Inventing Maternity: Politics, Science, and Literature,*

1650-1865. Ed. Susan Barash. Lexington, KY: UP of Kentucky, 1999. 57-85.

Laughlin, Rosemary M. "Anne Bradstreet: Poet in Search of Form." *American Literature*. 42. 1 (1970): 1-17.

Lutes, Jean Marie. "Negotiating Theology and Gynecology: Anne Bradstreet's Representation of the Female Body." *Signs* 22.2 (1997): 302-334.

Maragou, Helena. "The Portrait of Alexander the Great in Anne Bradstreet's 'The Third Monarchy.'" *Early American Literature* 23.1 (1988): 70-81.

Margerum, Eileen. "Anne Bradstreet's Public Poetry and the Tradition of Humility." *Early American Literature* 17.2 (1982): 152-160.

Martin, Wendy. "Anne Bradstreet's Poetry: A Study of Subversive Piety." *Shakespeare's Sisters: Feminist Essays on Women Poets*. Eds. Sandra Gilbert, and Susan Gubar. Bloomington, IN: Indiana U P, 1978.

—. *An American Triptych: Anne Bradstreet, Emily Dickinson, Adrienne Rich*. Chapel Hill, NC: North Carolina UP, 1984.

Mawer, Randall R. "'Farewell Dear Babe': Bradstreet's Elegy for Elizabeth." *Early American Literature*. 15 (1980): 29-41.

McElrath, Joseph R. "The Text of Anne Bradstreet: Biographical and Critical Consequences." *Seventeenth-Century News* 34 (1976): 61-63.

Mehler, Carol R. "Anne Bradstreet's House Fire: The Careless Maid and Careful God." *Studies in Puritan American Spirituality* (1995): 63-71.

Murphy, Francis. "Anne Bradstreet and Edward Taylor." *The Columbia History of American Poetry*. Eds. Jay Parini and Brett C. Millier. New York: Columbia UP, 1993. 1-15.

The New Testament of Our Lord and Saviour Jesus Christ with Psalms and Proverbs: King James Version. Nashville, Tennessee: Gideon, 1968.

Nichols, Heidi L. *Anne Bradstreet: A Guided Tour of the Life and Thought of a Puritan Poet*. Phillipsburg, NJ: P&R, 2006.

Oser, Lee. "Almost a Golden World: Sidney, Spenser, and Puritan Conflict in Bradstreet's 'Contemplations.'" *Renascence: Essays on Value in Literature* 52.3 (2000): 187-202.

Pender, Patricia. "Disciplining the Imperial Mother: Anne Bradstreet's 'a Dialogue between Old England and New.'" *Women Writing, 1550-1750*. Eds. Jo Wallwork and Paul Salzman. Meridian: The La Trobe University English Review: 18, (2001). 256.

Piercy, Josephine K. *Anne Bradstreet*. Twayne's United States Authors Series. Vol. 72. NY: Twayne, 1965.

Reed, Michael D. "The Prologues of Edward Taylor and Anne Bradstreet: A Psychoanalytic Reading." *Journal of Evolutionary Psychology* 18.1-2 (1997): 5-14.

Reid, Bethany. "'Unfit for Light': Anne Bradstreet's Monstrous Birth." *New England Quarterly: A Historical Review of New England Life and Letters* 71.4 (1998): 517-42.

Requa, Kenneth A. "Anne Bradstreet's Poetic Voices." *Early American Literature* 9 (1974): 3-18.

—. "Anne Bradstreet's Use of DuBartas in 'Contemplations.'" *Essex Institute Historical Collections* 110 (1974): 64-69.

Reuben, Paul P. "Chapter 1: Anne Bradstreet." *PAL: Perspectives in American Literature—A Research and Reference Guide.* <http://web.csustan.edu/english/reuben/pal/chap1/bradstreet.html> 30th Of Jan. 2009.

Rich, Adrienne. "Anne Bradstreet." *Major Writers of Early American Literature.* Ed. Everett Emerson. Madison: Belknap, 1972. ix-xx.

Richardson, Robert D., Jr. "The Puritan Poetry of Anne Bradstreet." *Critical Essays on Anne Bradstreet.* Ed. Pattie Cowell, and Ann Stanford. Boston: G. K. Hall, 1983.

Rosenfeld, Alvin H. "Anne Bradstreet's 'Contemplations': Patterns of Form and Meaning." *New England Quarterly* 43 (1970): 79-96.

Rosenmeier, Rosamond R. "'Divine Translation': A Contribution to the Study of Anne Bradstreet's Method in the Marriage Poems." *Early American Literature* 12 (1977): 121-35.

—. *Anne Bradstreet Revisited.* Twayne's United States Authors Series. Vol. 580. Boston: Twayne, 1991.

—. "The Wounds upon Bathsheba: Anne Bradstreet's Prophetic Art." *Puritan Poets and Poetics: Seventeenth-Century American Poetry in Theory and Practice.* Ed. Peter (ed. & pref.); Meserole White, Harrison T. (advisory ed.). University Park: Pennsylvania State UP, 1985. 129-146.

Saltman, Helen. "'Contemplations': Anne Bradstreet's Spiritual Autobiography." *Critical Essays on Anne Bradstreet.* Eds. Pattie Cowell and Ann Stanford. Crit. Essays on Amer. Lit.. Boston: Hall, 1983. 226-237.

Sargent, Ritamarie. "Poetry and the Puritan Faith: The Elegies of Ann Bradstreet and Edward Taylor." *A Salzburg Miscellany: English and American Studies 1964-1984.* Ed. Wilfried (introd.). Haslauer. Salzburg Studies in English Literature: Poetic Drama & Poetic Theory (PD), Salzburg, Austria. Series No: 27: 6.

Salzburg: Inst. fur Anglistik & Amerikanistik, Univ. Salzburg, 1984. 149-160.

Schweitzer, Ivy. "Anne Bradstreet Wrestles with the Renaissance." *Early American Literature* 23.3 (1988): 291-312.

Showalter, Elaine. *A Jury of Her Peer: American Women Writers from Anne Bradstreet to Annie Proulx.* NY: Alfred Knopf, 2009.

Stanford, Ann. "Anne Bradstreet." *Major Writers of Early American Literature.* Ed. Everett Emerson. Madison: Belknap, 1972. 33-58.

—. *Anne Bradstreet, The Worldly Puritan: An Introduction to Her Poetry.* NY: Franklin, 1974.

Sweet, Timothy. "Gender, Genre, and Subjectivity in Anne Bradstreet's Early Elegies." *Early American Literature* 23.2 (1988): 152-174.

Tichi, Cecelia. "The Puritan Historians and their New Jerusalem." *Early American Literature* 6. 2 (1971): 143-56.

Watts, Emily Stipes. "'The Posy Unity': Anne Bradstreet's Search for Order." *Puritan Influences in American Literature.* Ed. Emory Elliott. Illinois Studies in Language and Literature, Champaign, IL. Ser. 65. Urbana: University of Illinois Press, 1979. 23-37.

Wess, Robert C. "Religious Tension in the Poetry of Anne Bradstreet." *Christianity and Literature* 25.2 (1976): 30-36.

Whelan, Timothy David *"Mirror of Her Age": The Place of Human and Divine Knowledge in the Poetry and Prose of Anne Bradstreet.* Diss. University of Maryland College Park, 1989. *Dissertations & Theses: Full Text.* ProQuest. College Park, MD. 22 Jan. 2009 <http://www.proquest.com/> PDF file.

White, Elizabeth Wade. *Anne Bradstreet, "The Tenth Muse."* NY: Columbia UP, 1971.

—. "The Tenth Muse: A Tercentenary Appraisal of Anne Bradstreet." *William and Mary Quarterly* 7 (July 1951): 360.

White, Peter, ed. *Puritan Poets and Poetics: Seventeenth-Century American Poetry in Theory and Practice.* University Park: Pennsylvania State UP, 1985.

Wickers, Heather-Ann. "John Bunyan, *The Pilgrim's Progress* and Geoffrey Chaucer, *The Canterbury Tales.* The Author and his Reader: Christian Literature as Conversation." <http://www.literature-study-online.com/essays/bunyan-chaucer.html> August 2005.

Wilson, Douglas. *Beyond Stateliest Marble: The Passionate Femininity of Anne Bradstreet.* Nashville, TN: Highland Books, 2001.

Winebrenner, Kimberly Cole. *Anne Bradstreet: The Development of a Puritan Voice.* Diss. Kent State University, 1991. *Dissertations & Theses: Full Text.* ProQuest. Kent, OH. 22 Jan. 2009 <http://www.proquest.com/> PDF file.

—. "Bradstreet's Emblematic Marriage." *Studies in Puritan American Spirituality* 4 (1993): 45-70.

Winthrop, John. "From A Model of Christian Charity." *Anthology of American Literature.* 2nd ed. Vol. 1. Ed. George McMichael. NY: Macmillan, 1980. 62-72.

Wolter-Williamson, Jane Frances. *Anne Bradstreet's Construction of Predestination through Poetical Conventions and the Calvinistic Theology.*

Diss. Oklahoma State University, 1999. *Dissertations & Theses: Full Text.* ProQuest. Stillwater, OK. 22 Jan. 2009 <*http://www.proquest.com/*> PDF file.

Wright, Nancy E. "Epitaphic Conventions and the Reception of Anne Bradstreet's Public Voice." *Early American Literature* 31.3 (1996): 243-63.

INDEX

A

"Anne Bradstreet" (Stanford)   26, 41
Anne Bradstreet Revisited (Rosenmeier)
   27, 76
Arabella   19
"As Weary Pilgrim" (Bradstreet)   58-9,
   61-5, 69

B

Bartas: His Devine Weekes and Works
   (Sylvester)   22-3
Bradford, William   19
Bradstreet, Anne:
   inner conflicts of   14-15, 25-8, 56, 64,
      68, 75
   as a mother   21-3, 41
   overview of the life of   11-12, 14,
      17-18
   poetry of:
      conflicts in the   13, 40, 43, 49, 63
      influence of Puritanism in the   13,
         19-20, 25, 27
   spiritual journey of   57, 70
   tragedies in the life of   23, 36

Bradstreet, Simon   73
Bradstreet, Simon (Anne's son)   58
Bradstreet, Simon:
   as a leader   21
   marriage of   11, 17, 19
   poem for   50-1, 55, 69

C

Charles I   18-19, 21-3
Civil War   18-19, 22
"Contemplations" (Bradstreet)   37, 73-6
Cotton, John   21, 51

D

"Divine Translation: A Contribution
   to the Study of Anne Bradstreet's
   Method in the Marriage of Poems"
   (Rosenmeier)   69
Dod, John   17
Dryden, Erasmus   18
du Bartas, Sieur   22
Dudley, Anne *see* Bradstreet, Anne
Dudley, Thomas   11, 17, 19, 21, 26, 51

E

Elizabeth (Anne's grandchild) 23, 35-7, 50, 77
Elizabeth I 18
Ellis, John Harvard 43

F

"Flesh, and the Spirit, The" (Bradstreet) 25-9, 31-4
"Four Ages of Man, The" (Bradstreet) 22
"Four Elements, The" (Bradstreet) 22
"Four Seasons, The" (Bradstreet) 22
Franklin, Benjamin 20

H

Herman, Edward 19
Holland, John 19
Hutchinson, Anne 21, 51, 74

I

"In Memory of My Dear Grandchild Elizabeth" (Bradstreet) 35-7

L

Lodge, Thomas 18

M

Massachusetts Bay Colony 11, 15, 17, 22, 50, 74
Massachusetts Bay Company 19

May, Humphrey 19
Mayflower 19
Mercy (Anne's daughter-in-law) 23
Mercy (Anne's sister) 22-3

O

"Of the Four Humor" (Bradstreet) 22

P

Plymouth Plantation, The (Bradford) 19
Puritanism 11, 26, 41
   against female equality 51-2
   crisis in England 18-19
   in New England 12-13, 19

Q

Quaternions, The (Bradstreet) 22

R

Rosenmeier, Rosamond 27, 69

S

Samuel (Anne's son):
   birth of 21
   marriage of 23
   Puritanism lessons for 41
Sarah (Anne's sister) 23, 51
Seconde Sepmaine, La (du Bartas) 22
Sepmaine, La (du Bartas) 22
Several Poems 26, 37
Spenser, Edmund 18
Stanford, Ann 15, 33, 37, 54, 72, 76
Sylvester, Joshua 22

T

Tenth Muse Lately Sprung Up in America, The (Bradstreet) 23
"To My Dear and Loving Husband" (Bradstreet) 35-6, 50-5
Tyng, William 23

U

"Upon a Fit of Sickness" (Bradstreet) 21

V

"Verses upon the Burning of Our House" (Bradstreet) 35-6, 42-3, 49-50

W

Ward, Nathaniel 51
Williams, Roger 21
Wilson, John 21
Winthrop, John 11, 17, 19-20
Winthrop, John, Jr. 22
Woodbridge, John 23
Works of Anne Bradstreet in Prose and Verse, The (ed. Ellis) 43, 58

Y

Yorke, Dorothy 17

CPSIA information can be obtained at www.ICGtesting.com
Printed in the USA
BVOW041058171212

308026BV00002B/75/P